Daily Progress II

by Gary Stevens

This is the second of my Daily Readings books. It's aim is the same as the first, which is to bring a reading which feeds, stimulates and encourages, whilst trying to be the right length and depth of material.
Thank you to those who have helped and encouraged me in the writing of this book.

Gary Stevens

Autumn 2023

Table of Contents

The meaning of Jesus' name

Behold, the virgin shall be with child and bear a Son, and they shall call
his name Immanuel, which is translated "God with us".
You shall call his name Jesus for he shall save his people from their sins
Matthew 1: 23, 21

What's in a name?

In the Bible, names matter. They either maybe chosen by the parents as a tribute to God, or because of the circumstances of the child's birth. Or they may sense some trait in their child. And sometimes the child's name is given to them or changed by God. Abraham had his name changed, by God, from Abram (high father) to Abraham, father of many nations. Sarai, (meaning dominative), Abraham's wife, had her named changed by God to Sarah, (princess). Moses was named by the princess who took him out of the water – it means "drawing out", i.e., rescued.

Some names aren't over-complimentary (Mary means rebellious, Jael, wild goat, Deborah, ordered motion, i.e., a bee). My name is not a biblical name, but apparently means "son of a spearman" (which I am not!).

Why mention all this? Well, when I was young, I was constantly puzzled by one thing in the Christmas story. I'll share it with you. In Matthew 1:18-25 we read of the promise that the child the virgin would conceive would be given the special name Immanuel (v 23), but in fact he is called Jesus? Why is that so? The answer is that in the Bible, particularly in the Old Testament, names for God are what we call attributes: they describe something that God is. Hence, in Isaiah 9:6 this child – this Son - has some special names: which we will look at next time. But here, Jesus is called Immanuel which Matthew tells us means "God with us". Literally it translates as "with us is God". Jesus is God come to earth as a baby. He was and is a real human, who is also God. That is a mystery, but that is the plain teaching of the Bible.

That leads us to one last name: Jesus. Jesus is the same as Joshua: Jehovah saved. Why is he called that? The angel tells Joseph: he is to be called Jesus, for he shall save his people from their sins.

Isn't that amazing? There has been a baby born, sent by God the Father, to save his people from their sins. Who are "his" people? Are they good people? No. By definition they are at best sinners Jesus came to save. Are they religious churchy people? No. Jesus told the most religious people there ever were that their religion was useless. So, who are they? Callers: **For whoever calls on the name of the Lord shall be saved**. It is said twice in the Bible to give it emphasis: Joel 2, and Romans 10.

If Jesus came to save his people from their sins: what is sin? Sin is the breaking of God's law (I John 3:4). What is God's law? Jesus summed it up like this: *"You shall love the LORD your God with all your heart, with all your soul, and with all your mind. This is the first and greatest commandment. And the second is like it: You shall love your neighbour as yourself. On these two commandments hang all the Law and the Prophets."* Not one of us has kept those commandments for one single day, let alone from the moment we are born to the moment we die. But that is how high God's standard is, because that is what God is like: he is perfect (holy). He is love, and he is full of grace. Because he is holy, he cannot live with sin. He also knows we cannot keep the law, and rather than condemn all to hell, he sent his Son to take away our sin: Ann Gilbert, a Colchester hymn-writer puts it brilliantly, talking of Jesus:

> He knew how wicked man had been
> And knew that God must punish sin
> So out of pity, Jesus said
> He'd bear the punishment instead

That is why Christmas was so joyful to Mary, Elizabeth and Zacharias and the Shepherds. That is why the Wise Men trekked 1000 miles to see the baby. God's solution for the world had come, and they were part of it.

As we think of the Holy Child, I invite you in the name of Jesus to come to him, to call to him, to ask him to forgive you of your sin, to make you clean, and to make you his. He promises to accept you whoever you are and whatever you have done. What you must be is sincere.

Prayer: Lord, even if today is not Christmas day, help me to marvel at the fact that you came to this world as a baby, but also as God. Thank you that the reason you came was your immeasurable love for me. Amen.

4

Prince of the Four Names

His name shall be called Wonderful, Counsellor, The Mighty God, The Everlasting Father, The Prince of Peace

Isaiah 9:6

By the time this prophecy was given, the northern tribes of Israel had been taken into captivity by Assyria (Isaiah 8:4). The threat to Judah was real also, but the Lord in his mercy promised them deliverance. There had already been the "Immanuel" prophecy (7:14) but now the Lord expands his promise. That the Child was to be born in the land meant that God had a purpose for Judah which would come to pass. All of Israel would in fact one day bear witness to this Light of the world (9:2). God would become man, would come as a child. Yet he would have the government of God's people on his shoulders. He is a Royal person. He is the Prince of the Four Names[1]. This is the Jesus whom we worship and adore today.

Wonderful, Counsellor

Scholars differ as to whether the scriptures have in mind one title or two. But both ideas are possible. Jesus is Wonderful. He tells us that is his name in Judges 13:18. He is Counsellor. Jesus is the wisdom of God personified. See also Isaiah 11:2; Psalms 16:7, 33:11, Proverbs 8:14. He is the Wonderful One of Revelation 1, and the one in whom all the fullness of the Godhead dwells bodily (Colossians 1). But, If "wonderful counsellor is one Name (and my title says it is!) then we have a "wonder-counsellor. This emphasises the supreme - even supernatural - wisdom of he who is called the Word (John 1). In the darkness of Israel's spiritual rebellion, the one who was all wisdom, glory and knowledge was to dwell.

Mighty God

The name Immanuel already explains this man is divine. Now Isaiah states explicitly that he is Mighty God. The picture here is God being a warrior (Psalms 24:8; 50:1). In Psalm 89:19 Ethan tells of a conversation where

---

[1] This title was given by Alec Motyer

God (the Father) has given help to "one who is mighty," i.e. great David's greater Son. What was the fight he was going to engage in? Not against Assyria, nor any other superpower. When Jesus was born, Rome was in its pomp, but Jesus hadn't come to declare war on Rome with all its wickedness. He had come to make war on the prince of darkness, the enemy of your soul. He had come to strike the fatal blow to his head (Genesis 3:16). Jesus, the light had come to overcome the darkness that sin brings: to conquer sin, and death which is the result of sin. He was the mightiest of warriors.

Everlasting Father

How is it that Jesus the Son of God could have the title "Everlasting Father"? Well, literally the phrase is "Father of Eternity" and it refers to both Jesus "inhabiting eternity" (57:15), and to his care for his people. Vine comments *"He is loving, tender, compassionate, and all-wise Instructor, Trainer and Provider"* (see also Job 29:16; Psalm 68:5).

Prince of Peace

The mighty warrior God is also the Prince of Peace. Once sin, death and the devil are conquered there will be peace. This Prince brings, rules, and controls our peace. We have peace with God through our Lord Jesus Christ, now. When Christ returns the second time, there will be a kingdom set up which will be a kingdom of peace. No-one will ever invade that kingdom, for the enemy of our souls will be vanquished forever. God's people will not quarrel, neither with God, nor with each other! That is a tremendous thought, isn't it? But now Jesus gives us his peace. We can be free from guilt over our sin, free from the fear of death which used to enslave us. We can live a fulfilled life in peace.

What can we say to these things? If the Prince of the Four Names is for us, who can be against us? Yet one more thing should be said. God's ways are not as we expect them to be: this Prince of the Four Names was born in a stable and laid in a manger. He was poor,

uneducated, rejected, and crucified. How would you expect him to accomplish this supreme mission? He did so through suffering for us. He was the just who died for the unjust to bring us to God. Hallelujah, what a Saviour!

Prayer: Lord, these four Names tell me that you are so high and deserving of my worship. Help me to think about these names today and about how incredible it is that you stepped down to this world to save me. Amen.

A better covenant

And he is the mediator of a better covenant

Hebrews 8:6

A covenant is a pact between two people who bind themselves to do certain things. God made covenants throughout the scripture, with Adam, Noah, Abraham, Moses, David, and the children of Israel. But when Jesus came, he brought with him a new covenant, and as Paul writes, a "better" one.

What were the Old Covenants?

S. J. Hafemann' writes that there are three parts to a covenant with God. They are "Blessing, Command, and Promise. In Eden God <u>blessed</u> Adam with a paradise, <u>commanded</u> him not to eat from the Tree of Life and <u>promised</u> death if he did, and by implication life if he didn't. To break God's covenant, therefore, is to set aside his blessing, break his command and suffer the consequences. We see how that went for Adam, we see how that went for Israel, (carried off by Assyria never to return), and we see how that went for Judah: sentenced to 70 years in Babylon before God graciously brought them back. Once Adam and Eve sinned in the Garden and brought the curse of God upon mankind and all of creation, all the Old Testament covenants showed up how wicked man had become. However, Abram (as he was then) believed God's promise and "he counted it to him for righteousness". The Old Testament covenants were a foretaste of the New.

What is the New Covenant?

It is essential to state that the Bible is **one book.** There is not a different God or a different message in the Old Testament to the one in the New. All through the Old Testament the better covenant was promised. It starts in Genesis 3, and the picture of what it is like is added to as the Old Testament is written. The sacrifices of the Old pointed forward and were a shadow of the

New. Ezekiel tells us the New Covenant is one which won't be written on stone tablets, but on the heart. It is brought by Jesus, the Mediator, the Only Begotten Son of God. The New Covenant is based on <u>Blessing</u>: Jesus died and rose again. It is based on <u>Command</u>: believe in the Lord Jesus Christ. And <u>Promise</u>: if you believe in me, you will not perish (as those who will not believe) but have everlasting life.

Why is the New Covenant better?

It is better because it is based on better promises, a better sacrifice, and a better end. Israel had a physical covenant, although those who loved God and obeyed him are counted amongst the universal church. Jesus didn't come to bring about a new physical Israel, but an eternal church, a bride, a people who would love him, obey him, and trust him. The prize is not Canaan, but the new paradise of God, spent with God. Whilst it is true that God by his spirit dwelt in the midst of his people in the wilderness (as the tabernacle was in the middle and three tribes were on each of its four sides), it is even more true and wonderful that in the coming kingdom, God will dwell with his people. Whereas nobody could see God's face and live in the Old Covenants, in the new kingdom we shall see him face to face; we shall be like him for we shall see him as he is.

What does this mean for me?

You and I have the same opportunity now that all the heroes of faith had in the past. God offers his covenant to you. He does everything for your salvation. As in Eden, the provision is made, done, and finished. That is the Blessing. Now he asks you to obey his voice by repenting of your sin and believing in his offer of forgiveness and eternal life. That is his Command (you must be saved). Then you have a Promise to hold on to as you walk through this sin-filled, tear-stained world. That Promise is that this awesome, holy almighty and faithful God will never leave you, or forsake you, <u>no matter how it looks</u>. That is what hope is, trusting in the hard times, because of the evidence of God's grace in the past (at the Cross). Will you believe? Do you trust him? Have you entered into this wonderful covenant that God, out of mercy alone, has made for you?

Prayer: Father Jesus said, whoever comes to him he will not cast aside. Lord I come to you to save me. I ask you to forgive me for all my sin. Help me to trust whatever happens, you are in control, and nothing can snatch me away from your love and mercy. I worship you Lord. Amen.

12

I want to eat with you

With desire I have desired to eat this Passover with you before I suffer...
Luke 22:15

If you are a Christian, then you may well have taken part in the Lord's Supper many times. We are often solemnly told that we must examine ourselves before we come to make sure that there is no unconfessed sin

between us and the Lord, or between us and any other Christian. In fact, we are told to not take the table until we have put anything that may be amiss, right again. All that is correct and necessary, partly because if we are to have real communion it must be honest. If we are trying to fool

ourselves that all is well when it is not, then we have no place taking the bread and wine. If we are trying to fool the Lord, that is insulting, because he knows our hearts. Paul warns that the church **will not be** blessed if communion is dishonest. Perhaps it would be a good idea if we could create a time and space to make it as easy as possible for members to get together in honesty to confess our faults to one another and seek forgiveness.

The first Communion

The first Communion Service took place in an Upper Room in Jerusalem just hours before Jesus was crucified. It seems that thirteen people were present: Jesus and the 12 disciples. They sat down to eat, and whilst they were doing so, Jesus took a piece of bread, blessed it, broke into pieces and gave a piece to each disciple. Likewise he took a cup of wine, gave thanks, and told each one of them to drink. This was something, Luke tells, us that Jesus was fervently looking forward to doing. The question is: why?

14

The End of the Old and the Beginning of the New

You see there was no lamb in this meal. The Passover had been taken with all its symbolism for the last valid time. The Passover Lamb reminded the Israelites of their salvation from Egypt and their birth as a nation. But now it was ultimately fulfilled in what Jesus was about to do. He was about to die for the Jews and all others who would believe and reconcile them all to God. Israel was a type of the church, which the Lord was about to purchase with his own blood. Jesus had been on earth for 33 years or so. All now was coming to the end for which he came; to ransom his people. Not just Israel, but all who would believe.

When you take communion

Amongst all the other things that come to mind when you take communion: confession, worship, thankfulness, rejoicing and so on, let this one thought also come to mind: **Jesus wants to eat _his_ supper with _you_.** Of course, Jesus isn't eating and drinking physically, but he is present; he is head of the table. He desires to meet you there. Isn't that a thrilling thought? He desires to remind you that he loves you unquenchably. He desires to remind you that his blood really makes the foulest clean, and all your sins – even the disheartening "besetting" ones, can be, will be, and are forgiven. Take a moment to remember that, and to say thank you to him.

One day...

The communion table is a foretaste of Heaven. Have you ever thought about that? One day there will be no sin to confess, no-one to forgive or to reconcile with. The Old will have gone forever, and the New will last forever. It will be Paradise. There will not be bread and wine: there will be the Lamb on his throne, we will dwell with God in real and perfect communion.

So, if you are tempted to ask, what is the point of Communion? It is to remind you, not what a terrible sinner you are and how much you have failed since last time. It is to remind you that Jesus desires your company at his table. He desired it then with the 12. He desired with the

Laodiceans, he desires it with you, and he is looking forward to when you will not need it anymore because you will be with him forever. The man of Sorrows will bask in the happy Hallelujahs of his people, whom he has loved, ransomed and saved.

Prayer: Lord help me to see the Communion Table as a wonderful thing because you desire to sit with me and sup with me. Help me to always be so thankful for that moment. Amen

Defeated by Dandelions

Let us lay aside every weight and the sin which so easily ensnares us
Hebrews 12:1

Dandelions everywhere

If you read the first *Daily Progress,* you will remember my gardening skills weren't always successful. At the time when many of us were confined to home, I had too much time on my hands and began to be over-zealous with the lawn. Normally, it got mown sporadically but now I was out there every week with a surprised mower! But although it was tidy, I had never before noticed how many dandelions there were in it. They were everywhere. I went out and picked the heads off those the mower had missed. The next day there were dozens more, so I picked those off as well. The next day the same. I burned the heads off. I bought weed-killer and sprayed them. They kept growing. How did this happen? What did I do? The answer  was "nothing". I had not looked after the lawn, and it had gone wild all by itself. If I wanted to get rid of them, I would have to be out there every day until they are all gone.

Sins are like that

One of the good reasons for a time every day with the Lord, is that it gives an opportunity to stop and reflect on how we are doing in our Christian walk. When we are "too busy" to do this we don't notice bad habits creeping in and the "little sins" get in every aspect of our lives. Our language may become laced with words we ought not to use. Our hearts can become arrogant, or covetous, or dissatisfied with our lot. It doesn't take anything but laxness to let these sins grow, because the seeds are always there. In Song of Solomon 2:15 he laments how the "little foxes spoil the vineyard". How do we deal with these "little sins"?

Lay them aside

Well, that sounds very easy, lay them aside, but the picture Paul uses is that of a net that is caught around your feet. Trying to run anywhere let alone a race is impossible. A simple net made up of fairly thin fibres or strings can ensnare a big animal. So, it may be simple, but it's not easy. I could simply get down on my hands and knees and dig out every one of the dandelions; simple, yes; easy, no. How do we lay them aside: How do we disentangle from the irritating and baffling net? Simple, but not easy. We have to take them on. We have to decide that this sin is going to go. To use Solomon's illustration, the foxes have to be taken.

Feeding and killing

Going back to the lawn (and the dandelions); there needs to be a policy of feeding the grass and killing the weeds. Dig out what you can without leaving great holes in the lawn, putting on a weedkiller that will not harm the grass; picking off the heads before they turn to seed pods. It is a long job. So it is with sin. We need to identify it and maintain a constant war against it. Feed the soul with what is good, starve the sin of anything that encourages it to grow. As with the dandelions the war never ends.

At the root...

Dandelions have extremely long roots I have found out! The root is where it all happens. At the root of each sin there is a reason for its existence. That is not the same as an excuse. There is no excuse for sin, but there is a reason. When Paul lists all these sins in Romans 1, notice what he gives as the reason for all sins happening. This will surprise you: although they knew God, they did not glorify Him as God, nor were thankful. At the root of every sin is a lack of thankfulness to God; a belief that God has not given me what I want. That was Eve's problem. And so it is in every sin: stealing; adultery, coveting, sabbath-breaking etc. They all start with "if only...". So, to start rooting out the sins in your life, begin with making a conscious effort to thank God for all he is, all he has done, all he is doing and all he has in store. Thankfulness is the key to a walk that is unentangled by these "little sins". Give time every day to thank God, to be thankful. Start at mealtimes. Continue at the break and end of day. Look for opportunities throughout the day to be thankful. You are killing weeds with every thankful breath.

Prayer: Lord help me to see afresh all you have done for me, all you do every day, even in the trials of life, and all you have in store for me in Heaven. Help me to consciously say thank you and be thankful. Amen

The Axe Head

... it fell into the water.. he cried out: Alas, master, for it was borrowed
II Kings 6:1-7

I love the life-story of Elisha. To me he epitomises the Lord Jesus more than any other Old Testament prophet. Like Jesus, he takes time out for ordinary people too. He really was the people's prophet.

Encouragement in dark times

Elisha lived around 800BC. Israel was in a dreadful spiritual state. There had been no godly ruler in Israel for 100 years, God's word was set aside, and idolatry was on every corner. Worship of the Lord was largely abandoned by Israel, for God was left out of their thinking. War was never far away; famines kept occurring, but the king refused to follow God.

So, it is quite surprising to read in II Kings 6 of these "sons of the prophets". They were a band of godly men, who studied the word of God, under Elisha. Their numbers grew so much that one day they came to him to ask if he would go with them and help them build a new college to study in.

Guidance

So, the men sought guidance from the man of God, and because the Word of God was with him, they were seeking the guiding hand of the Lord himself. It is the great principle of guidance that before we lift a finger; before we write a heading down on the planning sheet, we take it to the Lord in prayer. Failure to do this is presumptuous and foolish. These men wanted the Lord to be in this venture, or they would not do it. Praise God they had great plans for the work; praise God also that they came and sought his will and his face in the matter. Not only did they ask for the word of the Lord, and seek the mind of the Lord, but they also sought the blessing and presence of the Lord in the venture. They asked for the man of God to go with them. They had the right desire; the right motive and they went about it the right way.

Now you might expect that such a venture: begun in such a way; done in the right way and for all the right reasons, would go well. But it doesn't. Disaster strikes, when through no fault of his own, this young man loses the head of his axe. It falls into the Jordan and is lost to sight. "Alas" he

cries in anguish. Not only can he not contribute to the work; not only has he wasted his time going out to the Jordan, but he is now in debt to the owner of the axe. Alas means "complaint". The simple plain truth is then as now, that when we embark upon a venture for the Lord, that sometimes things unexpectedly, inexplicably, and infuriatingly go wrong. What do we do then? Notice what the prophet does: he does the right thing. He cries out to the man of God – he cries in effect to God himself. *"Alas, master, it was borrowed. So, the man of God said, "Where did it fall? And he showed him the place. So, he cut off a stick and threw it in there; and he made the iron float. Therefore, he said, Pick it up for yourself. So, the young man reached out his hand and took it"*. It was yet another miracle that Elisha performed.

Sometimes prayer is from an anguished heart
You know, prayer hasn't got to be "perfect"; it has to be honest. That means that we may not use the "right words", if we are anguished, but honest, prayer goes straight to the heart of God. The axe head is going to fall off sometimes. When it does, turn **to** God and not **on** God. There is a reason why the axe head falls off; the enemy will always try and thwart God's work, big or small. and we need to ask God to turn it into something good for the Kingdom. We may not get the axe head back, but we will experience the blessing, help and leading of God in all our troubles. That, he promises. This story tells us that sometimes God surprises us when he acts in a way we could never anticipate. Our God is able to do abundantly, above all we ask or think. So, when the axe-head falls of, trust him, and ask him to help you. *"He who did not spare his own Son, but delivered him up … how shall he not with him freely give us all things… in all these things we are more than conquerors through him who loved us" Romans 8:32 & 37*

Prayer: Lord help me to trust you when things go wrong, even when I am trying to serve you. Help me to see that this is what happens in kingdom work, and in the ordinary Christian life. Help me always to turn to you in my despair and find your help. Amen

Isaiah's encounter with God

I saw the Lord, sitting on a throne… [the Lord said] whom shall I send, and who will go for us? Then I said, "Here am I, send me". And he said, "go…"

Isaiah 6:1, 8, 9

The three longest prophetic Old Testament writers are Isaiah, Jeremiah, and Ezekiel. They write amazing prophecies, and they were amazing men. But they were quite different men, with different ministries, and circumstances. I would like us to look at them in succession.

Isaiah's circumstances

Jewish writers believe Isaiah was of the noble classes, maybe even a cousin of the king. The Bible doesn't confirm that, but Isaiah knew the royal family well. He writes a biography of Uzziah, is well versed in the politics of his day and has ready access to the king and court. He is a great and fearless orator. His book is the second most quoted (after the psalms) in the New Testament and is named 21 times. The language is often poetic and hard to decipher but there are these rich passages which we know. Isaiah is quoted both at Christmas and Easter. His lot was mainly comfortable; he had the confidence of the king and had a long ministry. Hebrews 11:37 tells of those who were killed by being sawn in two, and the Jewish Talmud says this happened to Isaiah at Manasseh's command - we do not know for sure.

Isaiah's call

We are told exactly when Isaiah was called to serve God. it was in the year the long reigning and prospering king Uzziah died, in 740BC. Judah had known great stability over many years, but the next king was not of the same ilk. What would happen to the nation now? in this uncertain moment God called Isaiah to preach in a special way. He was privileged to see the Lord. But this encounter was so breath-taking Isaiah couldn't even describe it. There was no language rich enough; all he can do is describe the train of the robe of the Lord filling the Temple. This was a theophany –

a meeting with Jesus before he came to the earth (John 12:41). This sight was overwhelming, and Isaiah is struck by the purity and utter holiness of God. Immediately, he realises, with anguish, his own sinfulness. Isaiah, like his people, needs cleansing and so from the altar where a sacrifice has been made, coal is taken to cleanse Isaiah's lips and the first thing he says is to ask the Lord to allow him to be his messenger. And so, the Lord sends him to the people whom he had lavished his covenant love and provision upon, but who had turned away from him.

Isaiah's ministry

And so with such a wonderful encounter to sustain him, with such an awe-inspiring glimpse of the holiness and majesty and power of the Lord, to enrich his heart and soul, Isaiah volunteers to take God's word out to his people. But it is to be a thankless task. God's people didn't want to know. And although Isaiah did have the privilege of seeing God act in wonderful ways, particularly at the lifting of the siege of Jerusalem against the Assyrians, his message went largely unheeded. God's people loved their sins too much to let them go.

What has Isaiah got to do with me?

The encounter that Isaiah had with the Lord, shaped his life. He never forgot the astounding vision he saw of God's holiness, and it shaped his ministry. That raises a question; what is your concept of God? Is he the angry God; the loving God; the far-away God; the call-on-you-when-I-need-you God? Are you awed by his holiness; stunned by his mercy or is he someone you just cannot really trust? How we understand God, shapes who we are and how we live. For Isaiah, God was the holy, yet merciful God who loved his people with an endless forgiving and sacrificial love, and this shaped how he thought and how he spoke of God. Perhaps his concept of God is summed up in 43:3: *For I am the Lord your God, the holy one of Israel, your Saviour.* Read the early verses of Isaiah 6 and reflect for a moment on your concept of God and see if it matches up to Isaiah's. If it doesn't then seek the Lord afresh and ask him to show you what he is like. Read through Isaiah 40 and Psalm 104 and see God in his greatness and unchanging power, provision, and goodness. Because of what he is and what he has done, we can trust him at all times.

Prayer: Lord, please help me to have a right understanding of who you are, what you have done, and all that is laid up ahead for me. Help that understanding shape what I am, and how I serve you today. Amen

Jeremiah's Call

*Before I formed you in the womb, I knew you... I sanctified you... I
ordained you.*
Alas Lord I cannot speak...
You shall go to all whom I send you... for I am with you to deliver you...
Jeremiah 1:1-19

Jeremiah's circumstances

Jeremiah was a Levite from Anathoth in Benjamin's territory, a small town
about three miles north-east of Jerusalem. His youth was spent training
for the priesthood. It was his birthright and his joy, for only Levi's tribe
were priests. When he was 20, he would join his kinsmen in this sacred
and holy task. But before that happened, God stepped in. Whereas Isaiah
was in a secure city, enjoying the favour of the king and the comfort of the
court, Jeremiah lived through the dissipation, and destruction, of Judah as
they progressively turned their backs on God. He was hated. He was the
weeping prophet; in American literature to write a lament is to write a
jeremiad.

Jeremiah's call

Jeremiah was called to serve God in the 13th year of the godly Josia -
626BC - and he continued to serve until Judah was carried away to
Babylon in 586BC.

The Lord called Jeremiah by coming to him as a young man and telling him
that he had known him from before he was conceived. It reminds us of
Psalm 139, the beautiful psalm of God's love and omniscience. But for
Jeremiah, the message has a sting in it. God tells him to prophesy to
Judah, who has turned his back on God. Not only to them but to the
nations also. Jeremiah is amazed: he feels too young and insignificant: a
child, and his message will not be taken seriously. The Lord assures him he
wants him, and he is not to worry about opposition. As Moses found out,
the Lord was not to be dissuaded. Jeremiah had to lay down the
priesthood and live a difficult life of the prophet. He was not allowed to

marry (16:2), mourn, or feast. He felt his burden too great (12:1-2; 20:7-10) and longed to fly away (9:2) even cursing the day he was born (20:14-18). He had quite a different ministry to Isaiah, who experienced none of those things.

Jeremiah's ministry

Jeremiah is given visions to confirm his call. He is shown an almond tree. This is the first tree to blossom in January and is called the "wake-up" tree. In Hebrew, almond (shaw-ked) is akin to the phrase wake up (shaw-kad). Jeremiah is sent to wake up Judah for God has "woken up", so to speak, to his people's sins and has decreed the time is right to deal with them. Then Jeremiah is shown a boiling pot, facing away from the north. When the pot boils the broth is made and the drink is ready to be served. The cauldron stands for the Babylonian army that would come from the north, as Babylon was slightly east of Jerusalem so they had to march around the sea and come down from the north. The pot was ready, the army was ready, God's wrath was ready to be poured out on the nation. Judgement is coming, Thirty years later Nebuchadnezzar came, took away Jehoiakim and the nobility. Ten years after that the Temple and Jerusalem were destroyed.

Jeremiah was to face all sorts of trials. He was banished by his family: arrested, beaten, and imprisoned. He was put in a filthy, miry dungeon and left to die of starvation. He was called a traitor. He never saw his people repent, even after the captivity of Jerusalem and his forced exile to Egypt.

What has Jeremiah got to do with me?

Jeremiah reminds us of *what we are*: God's foreknown people who have a work to do. We may not feel brave or respected, nor that we have anything to offer God, but God has loved us with an everlasting love.

Jeremiah also reminds us of *what we are to be*. We are to be faithful, fearless, and confident in the Lord. Jeremiah, the timid man had to set his face as a flint. Scared he was, but he did the work God asked him to.

Like Jeremiah, we have an urgent message. The world won't like that message, and sadly nor do some in the church: yet, the true gospel must be preached, because it is **all** we have to offer the lifeless souls around us. Furthermore, we must adorn that gospel by loving God and loving one another. That is how God is glorified in us, and we are blessed in him. Jeremiah never forgot who he was, whose he was and what he had to do.

Prayer: Lord, to say thank that you have chosen me to be your child seems so lame, but here and now I give myself to you anew to do whatever it is you have chosen me to do. Help me to it with all my heart, in your strength and for your glory. Amen.

Ezekiel the watchman

Son of man, I have made you a watchman over the house of Israel,
therefore hear a word from my mouth and give them warning from me
Ezekiel 3:17

Ezekiel's circumstances

Ezekiel was a priest. But for him there was no temple to serve in because he tells us he is in exile by the River Chebar, a canal that watered Babylon. It is five years and five months since he was taken captive along with his king, and the former aristocrat is now a refugee living in a camp outside Babylon's great walls. Perhaps he knew young Daniel, who was in the king's palace (as far as he knew) enjoying Babylon's finest, whereas all his wealth, prospects, and career were over.

If he was tempted to envy Daniel, we are not told, but the tough lesson is that God calls each of us to our place, and we must be content with that, because the gifts and roles God asks us to play may have different attractions, but as in a body, each part is essential in the kingdom of God.

Ezekiel's call

The year is 592BC. Ezekiel is 30, and in this difficult set of circumstances, the word of the Lord comes expressly to him. He sees a vision of a whirlwind and four living creatures which represent God at work. After that he sees wheels which can move in any direction (God's omnipresence) and eyes (God's omniscience). God was saying that in this hopeless looking situation, he was at work; he was aware, and he was in control. God gave Ezekiel seven days to think over that message, and then he called him to be a watchman (he does it again in Chapter 33). A watchman was one who had to "peer forward," straining his eyes, so to speak, to see the danger coming. What was the danger? Not Babylon: they had arrived. It was whether Israel would at last repent. It was the danger to their own souls. Ezekiel's call to preach was not to warn of invasion as Isaiah's and Jeremiah's had been, his call was to see if they were ready to return to God, to his law and to his land.

Ezekiel's ministry
Ezekiel also has a peculiar vision to start his ministry. He is given a scroll to eat, which, to his surprise, is sweet. Yet, his ministry was a difficult one, because Israel was still not interested in God. Babylon was so impressive that God and his law may have felt out-dated and obsolete. Why listen to God? He has abandoned us. Judah had believed the cry of *"there'll always be a Judah, and Judah shall be free!"* Now, God had shown that sin brings judgement, and they had been severely judged. But now they were all for Babylon: so much so that only comparatively few returned after the captivity was over. Ezekiel's ministry was admired but ignored (33:30-33).

Yet Ezekiel's ministry was a rich one; 65 times he is quoted in the New Testament. Jesus used the epithet "son of man" for himself, aligning with Ezekiel's ministry, and used Ezekiel's type of the shepherd (Chapter 34) for himself. John uses his imagery in Revelation. Ezekiel may have thought at the end of his life that it was wasted, but in God's time Ezekiel has been greatly used of the Lord. He was obedient and faithful to his call, even though God asked him to do extremely hard and unpleasant things, including not publicly mourning the death of his beloved wife (24:15-18).

What has Ezekiel got to do with me?
If Isaiah embodies God's holiness, Jeremiah his eternal love, then Ezekiel embodies God's constancy. God is able to make the dead live (Ezekiel 37), and that Jesus has died and risen again is the message of the church. What part can we play in the spreading of that message? We can preach it, gossip it, love it, and live it out. Some ignored Ezekiel's message and some pretended to listen. Many people profess today to love Christ, but their actions betray him. Partly, it is because there are so few preachers who preach the unvarnished truth of the need for repentance, but also because on hearing about repentance their hearers do what Ezekiel's did: say it isn't for them. But if repentance isn't real, neither is eternal life with Christ.

Like Ezekiel, we must be faithful watchmen. We must warn that the Day of Judgement is appointed. The rebellious will perish eternally; the repentant will be saved eternally. This is the watchman's message: it was Ezekiel's ministry, and it is ours too. May we always be faithful to that task.

Prayer: Lord, I realise that to be a watchman is a difficult task, and maybe one I wouldn't choose. But as you gave it to Ezekiel, so you have given it to the church, and therefore, to me. Help me do this task today as best as I can, guided and led by the Holy Spirit. Amen.

Overcoming temptation

No temptation has overtaken you except such as is common to man, but God is faithful, who will not allow you to be tempted beyond what you are able, but with the temptation will also make the way of escape that you may be able to bear it

I Corinthians 10:13

As we've mentioned in our "dandelion" passage, sin easily entangles us, trips us up and hinders our Christian walk. But there are not just dandelions in my lawn; daisies, moss, and other weeds that I don't recognise, grow too. I happened to fixate on one. And we can do that in our Christian walk too. Like me, and my lawn, we fixate on one sin we believe we commit the most. You may have heard the phrase "besetting sin". It is one we seem to fall to most easily. But it maybe that this so-called besetting sin is not necessarily the one we commit the most, but the one of which we are most ashamed.

What is temptation?

James teaches us some blunt truths about temptation: *each one is tempted when he is drawn away by his own desires and enticed (1:14).* But *God cannot be tempted by evil, nor does he tempt anyone (1:13).* Go to Eden and compare it with I John 2:16-17. Eve saw that the fruit was good for food (lust of the flesh), it was pleasant to the eyes (lust of the eyes) and desirable to make one wise (pride of life). This does not change. The enemy aims to make it appear that what we are being tempted to do will satisfy a need that we must have. Doing this will give me something I have not got. And we go for it. But, in fact, what it is happening is we are saying to God; what you have provided for me is not enough. I want what you are "withholding" from me. It is ungrateful. It is insulting. It is why sin is so shocking.

Passing the opportunity up

God is faithful to us even though man and the world will be false. He knows about each and every temptation. In fact, God regulates this. He frustrates the work of the enemy who longs to see us fall big and fall away. What he uses to try and destroy us, the Lord allows to refine us, and build us up. We do not have to sin. It is something we choose to do in spite of all that God has done. The  Tyndale commentary tells us that Paul uses this word *escape* to paint a picture of a mountain pass. The picture is of an army being trapped in the mountains and seeing an escape route away from the enemy. God is in such control of our lives that every temptation is allowed, and yet has a way of escape.

How do I overcome temptation?

The first key is immediacy. Straightaway, go somewhere else; escape the source of the temptation. If you can't do that, pray that God will give you the strength to shun this enticing opportunity to grieve him.

The second key is preparation. You know you will be tempted. What armour can you put on to prepare for the fight? Ephesians 6:10-18 has the answer. The stronger you are in your daily walk and relationship with God, the more heightened your sense of sin will be and, in that dynamic, comes your strength. Avoid places where you will be tempted as much as you can, and, rather, go to those places where you will be strengthened.

In the end it comes down to a settled decision that today that you will stand up and fight. Passive, lazy Christians lose: pro-active Christians win. Like anything in life, it is about attitude. Today is a gift to you from God - how will you use it? Do you want to please the Lord, to make him smile? That takes effort. Pray, read the scriptures, and think carefully about what you have read. Seek to serve the Lord and his people. In these ways strength comes, and selfish desires recede. Sin is not just the breaking of God's law; it is serving myself and my selfish desires. Give today to God, and ask him to lead you away from temptation, strengthen when he leads you to it, and glorify him as you win some, at least, of those battles. Do not fixate on one "besetting sin", else, like me, you'll miss the daisies, the moss, and the buttercups. Instead, take a measured, whole-hearted approach to please the Lord wherever he takes you today.

Prayer: Lord, thank you that you always give me a way of escape from temptation. Help me to look for the escape routes and take them today. Help me today to overcome the temptation to sin and grieve you. Instead help me today to please and glorify you. Amen.

40

The message of the stars

When I consider the Heavens, the work of your fingers, the moon, and stars, which you have ordained, what is man that you are mindful of him, and the son of man that you visit him?

Psalm 8:3-5

Consider the Heavens

When you look at the stars on a dark night, when they shine their brightest, what is your reaction? "Wow" - is the one that most people have. There is something magical about them: their beauty, their far-away-ness, their vastness. And we are forced to wonder: how did they get there? How do they stay there? We feel so small and insignificant. So did David.

The moon and the stars are the works of your fingers

These Heavenly bodies are likened to blazing, rolling flames in Hebrew, and in Hebrew poetry are called "princes". David is describing their majesty as well as the physics. He tells us that God made them with his

fingers, a metaphor to show God's greatness. He uses a similar idea in Psalm 19:1 when he uses the word "handiwork" to describe the Heavens. It is as if God made them as a person would sew a small and intricate embroidery; beautiful but easy. How vast and unmeasurable God is! The Heavens with all their limitless majesty are but a piece of God's finger work. O Lord you are very great.

God considers me

One serious look at the stars tells me how small I am. The word "man" means mortal, and that reminds us how temporary we are compared to the Heavens. They have gazed down for thousands of years on millions of men and women doing their thing - and passing away like grass, whilst they have brightly blazed and scarcely changed. David wants us to get things into perspective. We are so taken up with our lives, cares, and battles as if they were of some importance, but in the grand scheme of things we are unimportant, transient, finite, and so small.

God marks me out

But, before we get down-hearted, David tells us we are not insignificant to God. He, the one who has made all things and transcends them, marks us out. That is what being mindful means. God knows us, recognises us, marks us. It reminds me of school and how the headmaster knew my name, and probably for the wrong reason! But God is not distant, unfeeling, or uncaring. He has not created the universe and then walked away without a care. As the other verses in the Psalm teach, God cares about his creation. He rules it and by his power all things exist and continue to exist. But man plays a part in this: in verse 6 we read that God has given man a job to do, to look after the world he has made. For that work mankind is accountable.

What does this Psalm teach me?

Not only does God take notice of us, but he lives with us. Furthermore, this Psalm points forward to the ultimate visit and the ultimate visitor. Just at the appointed time, Christ was sent into the world to be the Saviour (Galatians 4:4-5) and he died for us (Romans 5:6). There is a day appointed when he will return (Acts 17:31), wind this old world up like a worn-out coat, and create all things new.

The last thing is, notice how the Psalm begins and ends: *O LORD, or Lord, how excellent is your name in all the earth.* In the psalms it is always useful to look at the names the writer uses for God. The first LORD is Jehovah, the eternal one, and the second is Adonai, the master or divine owner. Our God, that we believe in and trust for our eternal salvation, has revealed himself to the world through his creation, of which the Heavens form such a striking part. The stars don't tell the future, as foolish people think, but they tell a story, a story about the wonderful God who made them, keeps them burning, and allows us to miraculously see their light.

He is all-powerful, almighty, and yet loving, caring, and providing for us every day. The stars tells us of God's constant love and power, and they should drive us to worship the one who loves and died for us on the Cross that we might live with him for ever. O Lord, how excellent, how famous, how precious is your name to your people throughout the world.

Prayer: Lord, I worship you for your greatness, your kindness and your daily provision and care. Thank you that whenever I look up, I can be reminded of these wonderful truths. Help me to do that today. Amen.

A surprising story

As he was going out on the road, one came running, knelt before him,
and asked Him, Good Teacher, what must I do to inherit eternal life?
Mark 10:17-25

This story contains so many surprising_things, there is scarcely room to fit them in. It is the story of the rich young ruler, and it is told in the gospels of Matthew, Mark, and Luke. That shows how important it is.

A surprising start

One day, Jesus starts off down the road for Jericho, when suddenly, he hears panting breath and footsteps behind him, and he turns to see a young man running towards him. But this is no ordinary man - this is a ruler of a local synagogue. He is dressed in fine clothes, for he is rich. Then he does something quite unexpected: he gets on his knees in front of everyone, and asks Jesus, *Good Teacher, what must I do to inherit eternal life?*

A surprising conversation

Firstly, the young man was asking the hardest question to the only one he thought had the answer. Jesus takes him straight to the Law. Confident of his ground, the young man tells Jesus that he has kept the Law from his youth. He is neither arrogant nor boasting here. He has lived a moral honest life and Jesus, who knows all things, doesn't question that. But, then in a wonderfully tender moment, we read Jesus looking at him, loved him. Jesus saw him as he was, a sinner, but he loved him. Jesus also gives him the answer he craved. To the young man's surprise, Jesus puts his finger uncomfortably on his weak spot. *One thing you lack: Go your way sell what you have, give to the poor and you will have treasure in Heaven, and come take up the Cross and follow me.* In saying this, Jesus knew perfectly well he was asking this Pharisee to do what was forbidden by rabbinical law.

A surprising twist

What an offer! The ruler knew that Jesus was something exceptional. By now, Jesus' ministry and reputation were well established. He was known and acknowledged, even by the Sanhedrin, as a teacher come from God (John 3:2). He had raised a dead girl at Capernaum, raised a dead boy at Nain, and fed multitudes with a few loaves and fishes – twice. His powers were very publicly demonstrated. This is the greatest man to walk in Israel and he is asking this young man to join him.

But the young man doesn't. He gazes into his own empty heart, gazes into the face of the only one who can save him, and trudges away in sorrow. He could not bear to give up all he had to follow Jesus Christ, the Messiah.

One more surprise

The disciples were bystanders to all this, and we read that they were literally struck dumb with amazement. Surely the rich, the moral, the pillars of society are saved by their virtue? *You only get rich by being good*, was their reasoning. Jesus states it is impossible for any trusting in riches to be saved. That camel will go through the eye of a needle first. Jesus doesn't chase after the young man. Even though he loved him, he let him go.

We all want to believe that we can contribute to our salvation. Rich people in vain point out how much they have given to charity, or how good they have been in some way. But Jesus says "no". We are saved by doing what Jesus tells the young ruler to do:

Sell all you have – this means get rid of everything that hinders you from being saved. Jesus, the Lord, must come first.

Give to the poor -the principle here is that what we have should be used in the work of the kingdom (gifts, talents etc). His work comes first.

Have treasure in Heaven – where your treasure is, your heart will be also. What you cherish is what you will work to keep. What we want above all is to be in the Paradise of God, where all is peace, perfection, and joy.

Come, follow me – eternal life starts now. Obedience and a desire to show our faith by the way we live starts now. Entrance to the kingdom has all been arranged for us, but we show our faith and hope by the way we live. Follow Jesus today and every day. Seek to please, obey, and honour him. That is what following is.

Prayer: Lord, help me today to take up your Cross, to be dead to my own ambitions, and to live for you. Help me to follow you wherever you lead me. Amen.

48

Entrusted with the gospel

But as we have been approved by God to be entrusted with the gospel,
even so we speak, not as pleasing men, but God who tests our hearts.

I Thessalonians 2:4

I imagine that your view of preaching is probably shaped by the preachers you've heard. Don't we often focus on the preacher's mannerisms, the sermon length and how "interesting" he was, rather than the message he preached?

First things first

A preacher, says the Bible, must be a man who is **entrusted** with the gospel. He is appointed by the Lord to preach the whole truth of God. Jesus appointed the first preachers (Luke 6:12-16), after a whole night of prayer. Just think of that: the Son of God spent the whole night in prayer with his Father before deciding whom he would send to preach. That alone shows the importance the Lord attaches to this task. Later, he would send out 72 preachers to cover the country of Israel, so he appointed 60 more (Luke 10:1-24). Those who are entrusted with the gospel are sent out by the Lord.

Who is entrusted with the gospel?

In the New Testament only men were called and spoken of as preachers. In these days of political correctness, the idea of only men as preachers is scorned, but nowhere in the scriptures are women allowed to preach in a congregation, and Paul's words are **not** cultural but creational (I Timothy 2:12-15). A woman simply is not called to preach..

A careful reading of I Timothy will show that preaching is not a casual thing you do because you feel the urge, but a calling from the Lord, which involves great sacrifice. It is something you give your life to, and you may suffer for it. James tells his brothers that a preacher will be subject to stricter judgement by the Lord, and, you can be sure, extra opposition by Satan, who strives maliciously to prevent the true gospel being preached.

What is the gospel?

The gospel is a message from God for mankind. All are to hear it, and all are commanded to believe it. He who believes will be saved from Hell, and he who refuses to believe is in fact condemned already (John 3). So, it is a serious task. The preacher must represent God and his message accurately, faithfully, and honestly. He must not add to it, nor hide away anything of it, else he corrupts the sacred truth and the sacred trust. In short, the gospel is in John 3:16. In Eden our first parents Adam and Eve sinned and brought sin and death with  it into every one of us. we are naturally dead in trespasses and sins (Ephesians 2:1). We are all unable therefore, to save ourselves as dead men are helpless to breathe. Jesus, God's Son, lived a perfect life and offered himself as a perfect sacrifice to God paying the penalty of sins. That sin offering needs to be credited to us.

The gospel is hard to preach and hard to accept

Why is this so? Because we must come ashamed of our sin and cast ourselves on the mercy of God. Jesus illustrated it best when he talked about the repentant tax-collector (a man hated by everyone for his wickedness) who came to the back of the temple, with his eyes on the floor, and beating his breast he pleaded, "God have mercy on me, a sinner". With that simple act of faith, he went home a justified man.

It is hard to accept we are sinners, and it is hard to preach to others telling them they are sinners too. But without the sickness being identified, there will be no felt need for a cure. We must be honest and truthful; everyone needs Jesus, and all who come like this man, will be accepted by the mercy of God as he counts his Son's sacrifice as their righteousness.

But maybe you are not a preacher. Fair enough, but if you are a Christian, you are a witness to the truth that has happened to you, and you have a duty too to tell others of the great things the Lord has done for you. You have a testimony, a story of how you were saved. No-one can take that away from you, so share that good news with all you can. That will not be easy, but it is the greatest news you have. No doubt someone shared it with you, now you share it with other people, whilst there is time to do so, and may God bless you as you do. In that sense all of us are entrusted with the gospel. Will you repay that trust today?

Prayer: Lord, help me today to share my story. If you are calling me to preach, please make that very clear to me and others also. Amen.

Lord, open his eyes

And Elisha prayed and said, Lord, I pray, open his eyes that he may see
II Kings 6:17

Elisha is on the national stage again, in this curious story. It isn't that long since God healed Naaman of his leprosy. The gratitude that the Syrian king felt with his commander back did not last long. He decided to raid Israel again. Since the Assyrian's were on the march again, he couldn't afford a major invasion. He sent raiding bands into Israel to grab what he could.

The Divine spy

Elisha told the king what Ben-Hadad was planning. The Israelite king heeded the warnings and Ben-Hadad was at first frustrated, then furious and then foolish. As raid after raid was thwarted it became clear that Jehoram was being warned, but by who? It had to be a traitor, a spy. Yes, but no ordinary spy; it was the Lord himself, through this same man Elisha. Ben-Hadad, at this point should have stopped and reflected on what was happening; he knew that this God had cleansed Naaman; he had been defeated by this God (via Ahab) twice in supernatural defeats (I Kings 20). Here was a warning to him; God can see all you do, but instead of humbling himself and worshipping the Lord as Naaman was doing, he decides to send a great army to Dothan to capture Elisha, and silence God.

The Divine scene

Imagine Elisha's poor servant when he wakes up and starts his "ordinary" day. He looks out of the window and in sheer amazement gazes at horses, chariots, swordsmen, and the glittering array of armour shining in the morning sun. Today, I die, he thought, and rushes to Elisha. "Alas, my master! What shall we do? But, to his surprise, Elisha doesn't panic. He calmly surveys the scene and tells his servant not to fear. Elisha could see what the servant couldn't, and his perspective of God controls how he acts. He sees the horses and the army of Syria, but he also sees the "divine scene", the angelic host. *"Open his eyes Lord"*, he prays, *"and let him see it as it really is"*. And the Lord opens the servant's eyes. An army of horses and chariots of fire are on guard around Elisha. What an insight into the spiritual world the servant is given. This is not how it looks but how it really is.

The Divine salvation

Elisha, in the power of the Lord, saves his people from their enemy. To do so he uses courage and guile. He asks that the Syrians be smote with blindness, not physical blindness else they could not travel the 12 miles to Samaria, but the same type of impaired vision that the two on the Emmaus road had. They could physically see Jesus but were kept from recognising him, until the Lord opens their eyes again. See the king of Israel almost dancing with delight as cries out to Elisha: "My father, shall I kill them? Shall I kill them?" Worldly wisdom says take your revenge on your enemies, but Elisha, prefiguring the command of Paul, says no. Instead feed them, water them, and let them go. He showed mercy, and it was the end of the raiding bands, the ambushes and the harassment. It was for Israel and for Syria a divine salvation.

Seeing is believing?

It is often said that seeing is believing, but the Bible teaches this is not the case. You and I are called to walk by faith and not by sight. This fact is seen over and over in this chapter. God dwells in an eternal realm, and that realm is usually hidden from our sight, for we could not bear to see it. The spiritual world is right alongside the material world - a bit like those one-way mirrors in the shops. You may get an occasional glimpse behind them, but they can see your every move. We read: There is no creature hidden from His sight, but all things are naked and open to the eyes of Him to whom we must give account (Hebrews 4:13). Psalm 139 says: When I awake, I am always with you. Jesus said I am with you to the end of the age; God vowed to Joshua (1:9): Be strong and of good courage; do not be afraid, nor be dismayed, for the LORD your God is with you wherever you go.

Elisha knew that God saw everything, was with him everywhere, and that all men need his mercy. Only God can give sight to the spiritually blind. Only God can save. We need to pray constantly; Lord open their eyes.

Prayer: Lord, today, I pray for those I know who are not Christians. They are spiritually blind. As I name them before you, I pray that you would open their eyes as you opened mine. Thank you, Lord. Amen.

57

Life's guiding principle

For those who honour me, I will honour, and those who despise me shall be lightly esteemed.

I Samuel 2:30

Eli was the priest of God at Shiloh, where the people of God came to worship him. To be such a priest was the highest privilege, but with high privilege comes great responsibility and accountability (James 3:1). Whilst Eli was a godly man, his sons were wicked. Although Eli knew this, he did  not discipline them as he should have. God said that he put his sons before the Lord. Their wickedness was so great, that God declared to Eli, that he would take away the family birthright to serve him in the priesthood. This finally came to pass some years later at the beginning of Solomon's reign (I Kings 2:27). By refusing to deal with his sons as he should Eli, was despising the Lord's name, his holiness, and his law. See I Samuel 3:12-14

The Christian life is governed by principle

In life there are things that are clearly right and wrong. We see that clearly in the Ten Commandments where God reveals his laws, his standards, and his character. Murder, adultery, and theft are clearly wrong. And I emphasise, those laws will still be in force until the Lord comes again.

In other spheres too there are rules that God has. Eli was a priest. The priests were clearly instructed on how to perform their duties and order their lives. Sadly, Eli did not do this.

But there cannot be a rule for everything, nor a guidebook which lists answers to every problem, so the question remains, how do we know what to do when there is no explicit answer? We work it out using the principles in God's word. One question, for example, is how to use the Lord's Day. The answer lies in another question: is what I want to do, whether it be shopping or playing sport, honouring the Lord? Obviously not, so don't do it.

What about a new job, or house, or going out with someone on a date? The answer comes by asking the same question: will doing this bring honour to the Lord? Will he pleased to find me here? Some might say; this does neither, but we cannot be neutral Christians; we are to actively and pro-actively seek the Lord's glory in all we do. In this way we "honour God". In all things the Lord is looking on our heart to see its motives.

Does this promise "work"

Let me give you a small example. A Christian football league played on Saturday mornings. Some other people started a Christian league on a Sunday. They invited the Saturday league to join them, but the league declined citing this verse. A certain animosity came from the Sunday league, who said that they had the better league, the better players and theirs would last longer. As a result, the two leagues met in a match (on a Saturday) and the Saturday league won 7 – 0. Soon after the Sunday league disbanded citing a lack of players. Those who honour me I will honour.

I'm sure you have other more serious examples of this happening in churches, in individual lives and maybe even your own life.

But there is a cost

However, making the hard choice costs. That Saturday league at one point had four teams! Was it even a league? If we do whatever it takes to honour God and put him first, it will cost. We may lose a job or a promotion because we will not work on Sundays, or it may cost a relationship. It may cost you friendships, even of Christians, who do not share your principle. But God sees; God knows. In his time, you will look back and see that he has also honoured you, and it is usually in a surprising, but clear, way.

Make the hard choice

Now we must make the hard choice. What is it to be? Will it be popularity, material gain, promotion, a bigger circle of friends, to name a few? Or will it be possible isolation, poverty, and criticism? The narrow path that the Lord spoke of (Matthew 7:14) remains a narrow path, right until the end, but at the end is the joy for which you chose that path in the first place. Live your life with the principle in mind that in all you do you will do it specifically with aim of honouring God.

Prayer: Lord, please give me a heart with decides to put you first in all things. When I am in doubt as to what to do, give me a heart which unashamedly seeks to honour you in my decisions. Amen.

Jesus is the Lamb of God

Behold the Lamb of God who takes away the sin of the world

John 1:1-18, 19-36

In the first Daily Progress, we looked at John calling Jesus the Word of God. John's gospel is about proving and convincing us that Jesus is the Son of God and that by believing in him we will have life in his name. The phrase "of God" is a Hebrew idiom which denotes that the thing spoken of is from God. John takes it to another level by using this idiom to flesh out

his thesis that Jesus is the eternal, co-equal Son of God. In this verse John the gospel writer quotes John the Baptist when he uses this title in a family of titles to describe Jesus. Jesus is "of God" – he is divine. He is the Lamb of God.

Perfect Lamb

God gave instructions about a lamb being sacrificed in Exodus as part of the sacrificial law: *every man shall take for himself... a male... without blemish*. It had to be perfect and male. In proclaiming Jesus was the Lamb of God, John the Baptist was telling his listeners that Jesus is perfect. He is a male of absolute perfection. The Father agreed: this is my beloved Son in whom I am well pleased (Matthew 17:5). He never gave this testimony about anyone else. Nor could he. Jesus is the Perfect Lamb of God.

Provided Lamb

Abraham was told to sacrifice his son (Genesis 22:1-2). This was his "only son, whom you love". The words resonate with the paragraph above, It seemed unbelievable for God to ask this, but Abraham believed that God would provide a lamb, or that God would restore his son to life. God did provide the lamb for Abraham, foreshadowing he would provide a Lamb for his people too. Thus, the Lamb of God is a lamb that God provides.

Protecting Lamb

When Jewish minds thought of a lamb in a sacrifice, perhaps they would think first of Passover. If ever a sacrifice resonated with the whole nation, this was it. In Egypt Israelites gathered in their homes, sacrificed a lamb, and put the blood on the top and sides of the door. Whoever was inside the house would be safe. Whoever was not in a house covered by this lamb's blood would see their firstborn die. It was the blood of protection, and it was commemorated yearly as a feast of sacred joy and profound thankfulness. For the Baptist to describe Jesus as the Lamb of God was to portray him as the One who would also provide protection from God's destroying angel. Jesus is the Lamb who protects us from judgement.

Passive Lamb

Jesus submitted to being the Lamb of God. He was the Silent lamb of Isaiah 53:1-7. He was a passive Lamb: he did not protest or try to escape. When praying at the Garden of Gethsemane, Jesus says to his Father, *"not my will but yours be done"*. When the guards come to arrest him there, he says *"this is your hour"*. He told Peter to put up his sword and healed Malchus' the High Priest's servant's ear when he heroically tried to defend him. Jesus allowed them to take him. This passive Lamb was led away to be slaughtered for the sins of the world. Jesus was the Passive Lamb of God.

Perpetual Lamb

In the life of Israel, a lamb was slain every morning and every evening. It was a perpetual offering maintaining fellowship with God. Ryle writes: *He was the true Lamb to which every lamb in the morning and evening sacrifice pointed* (see Exodus 29:38-46). It was also a lamb of remembrance and a lamb of consecration. Israel, having been bought (redeemed) from Egypt now belonged to God and were wholly his. Jesus in dying for us, does the same. We have peace with God through the Lord Jesus Christ. The Lamb died so that the people could constantly be in the presence of God, have fellowship with God and live wholly for God. It is an ever-effective lamb. Where Israel used many, God used one. Jesus is our perpetual Lamb of God.

Can you see how rich in meaning this little phrase is? Jesus is the Lamb of God who takes away the sin of the world. But, John says, "Behold". Have you looked steadfastly at Jesus the Lamb of God? Has he taken away your sin? Is he your Personal Lamb? Do you know him and love Him? Today, remember, reflect, and rejoice in the loving sacrifice of Jesus the Lamb of God just for you.

Prayer: Lord thank you that in Jesus all the types and shadows of the ceremonial law are fulfilled. Help me to think on these things. Amen.

Arise, and worship the Lord

Then God said to Jacob, "Arise, go up to Bethel and dwell there; and make an altar to God, who appeared to you when you fled from the face of Esau your brother." And Jacob said to his household and to all who were with him, "Put away the foreign gods that are among you, purify yourselves and change your garments".

Genesis 35:1-2

The material for today's reading comes from a sermon entitled "Full Spiral" preached by Pastor James Young of Hillfields Church, Coventry. There was much that he said, but I want to focus on one thing: *"we should arrive at whole-hearted worship"*.

A command to worship
You and I, if we are Christians need to arrive at this place of whole-hearted worship. For Jacob it meant literally to rise up and travel. He left Shechem and travelled a few miles south to Bethel where he had had encountered God, who was above a great ladder that he saw reached up to Heaven. But uniquely, God told Jacob to build an altar. Normally the patriarchs built an altar at their own desire. Here God tells Jacob, to rise, go and build. So, he was commanded to worship.

A worship that was deeper than before
Jacob had years before been to Bethel and met God there. He had vowed then that if God kept his promise to preserve and prosper him then when he returned, he would worship and serve the Lord. Now was the time to fulfil that vow. But Jacob returned a different man. When he left the family home, he did so because he had cheated and deceived his own brother. He was fleeing for his life. He had heard about God from his parents until Bethel. Now he had had an encounter with the living God. That is why he named the place Bethel (house of God). But even so his worship was based on a very shallow understanding of the Lord. Since then, he too had been deceived and cheated. Yet, he had known God's blessing. He had made peace with Esau. He had even wrestled all night

long with the Lord and prevailed (Genesis 32:22-30). God implicitly reminds him of all this and of how far he had come in verse 1. Jacob's worship was now based on a deeper knowledge and experience of and gratitude to the God who chose him and loved him.

Two necessary steps to worship

Before Jacob and his household could worship God there needed to be some serious preparation. The first thing was repentance: Jacob instructs them solemnly to *"put away their idols…"*. This is repentance in action. Clear out the idols. Jacob buried all of them under a big tree. We must also bury ours: get rid of everything you love more than Jesus. There is a solemn and terrifying passage in Matthew 7:21-22. The "Lord, Lord" you cry to on the last day needs to match the "Lord, Lord" you worship here on earth.

The second thing Jacob needed was faith. In faith they had to purify themselves. They would no doubt come to offerings later, but first they were told to change their garments. This symbolised a change of heart – a pure heart - necessary for worship. They needed garments of righteousness, and so do we. Paul writes in Romans 13:14 that we should clothe ourselves in the Lord Jesus Christ. Put our faith in him. Put on his righteousness. That is how we can enter God's presence at all.

Arrive at whole-hearted worship

Like he did with Jacob, God commands you and I to worship him. Worship is a continuous act of faith. We are to worship him because of who he is, for what he has done, is doing and will do for us. There is so much to worship God for. But we need to continue the cycle of repentance and keeping on burying our idols, for they don't magically disappear on their own. We need in faith to continually put on the Lord Jesus and his righteousness. Worship is not just about going to services of worship (although that is vital), but to continuously live a life of worship. Each time we do this our worship will grow richer and deeper and we arrive at the place of whole-hearted worship. We are told to delight ourselves in the

Lord. Worship is joyful, heartfelt, grateful, humble, marvelling at the goodness, kindness, and love of God. Worship is reverent homage to the most High God who sent his Son the Lord Jesus to die for us, taking away our filthy rags of self-righteousness and giving us his white robe of righteousness to wear forever. Rise up and worship the God who has preserved your life and given you a place in his heart and his kingdom. This is worship and this is enough to live by.

Prayer: Lord, today help me to understand what worship is. It is more than a feeling. It is an act of heartfelt praise and thanks for who you are and what you have done. Help me to arrive at whole-hearted worship. Amen.

68

Jesus is the Son of God

I have seen and testified that this is the Son of God.
Rabbi: You are the Son of God...

John 1:1-34 and 49

We come today to a third title of the Lord found in John 1: the Son of God. This title is given by three witnesses: John the Baptist, Nathanael, and Mary.

John the Baptist

John saw the divinity of Jesus affirmed with his own eyes. He saw the Holy Spirit descend on him in the form of a dove in fulfilment of the promise that God gave to him. John was the last prophet of the Old Testament, the last man to point towards the Lord's coming. His job was first to announce he was coming and then he had the greatest privilege of all the prophets by announcing Jesus was here.

In quoting the Baptist, John the writer reminds his readers that there is no-one – not even the Pharisees - who would deny that John was a man sent by God, and therefore it follows that he was telling the truth. John was one of the greatest and godliest of men, and John the writer is saying that we should treasure his memory and believe his message. The Baptist declared unequivocally that Jesus Christ is the Son of God and paid for it with his life.

Nathanael the disciple

We do not know very much about Nathanael of Bethsaida. He was a good friend of Philip. He was a godly man who knew the scriptures well enough to look for the promised Messiah. He didn't know Jesus personally, but he knew the town he came from, and that no prophecy was written about Nazareth being the town where the Messiah would come from. What he didn't know was that Jesus had been born in Bethlehem as the prophets had spoken, but was raised in Nazareth, so fulfilling in an unexpected way another prophecy (he shall be called a Nazarene).

What convinced Nathanael so quickly that Jesus was divine? How did he know that this was the Messiah? Jesus knew him inside out and, with a sentence, convinced him that he had read his mind and thoughts. Nathanael knew that only he and God could have known what he had been saying or doing under the fig tree and so Jesus had to be divine. Now, again ask yourself, why would a man who had never met Jesus suddenly stop all that he was doing and being and instead follow and serve a man who appeared to have nothing at all to lure him with? The answer can only be that Nathanael was convinced that Jesus was divine, so convinced he gave up everything, left it all behind to follow Jesus. This he did until the day he died.

Mary the mother
Mary alone knows that Jesus is the Son of God. She alone knew of the Jesus conception. The disciples didn't; Joseph didn't – he had to accept the angel's word on trust. The only person who could really vouch for the Virgin Birth: the Immaculate Conception; the work of the Holy Spirit upon her life, was Mary. And so Mary is brought into the narrative; not because she says anything publicly, but because here she affirms in this story what the angel had told her (Luke 1:35). "Whatever he says to you do it". This shows her faith even though she had never seen him do anything miraculous.

And so, Jesus does the miracle. Without fuss, or drama Jesus shows his power over nature. John has already written that "All things were made through him and without him nothing was made that has been made". Now he proves it. Jesus changes one substance into another by a word. It is a staggering miracle to us – a word of power to him.

Thus, John has his three witnesses: in scripture a threefold emphasis is our equivalent of saying something is true in the strongest of terms. Jesus is the Son of God: the Baptist declares he has seen the Holy Spirit descend on him: Nathanael the Apostle declares that Jesus could read his heart without ever knowing him before; and Mary by her actions shows that she knows full well that her son is the Son of God even before he starts his ministry of signs, wonders and teaching.

Application

Focus on the phrase that Mary uses: *"whatever he says to you do it"*. What does Jesus ask us to do today? If Jesus is the Son of God, we must follow him and obey him. Three things stand out that he asks us to do: to love one another, to pray without ceasing, and to do all to his glory. Think about what that might look like in your life today.

Prayer: Lord, thank you that I can talk to you, the Son of God. Help me to follow you in faith, love and obedience. Help me to pray without ceasing, to love my neighbour and to seek your glory in all I do today. Amen.

Three choices

Abram said to Lot, "Please let there be no strife … Please separate from me. If you take the left, then I will go to the right…" Lot lifted his eyes and saw all the plain of Jordan, that it was well watered … Then Lot chose for himself all the plain of Jordan, and Lot journeyed east.

Genesis 13:8-9

Abraham's choice

Abraham was from Ur, now called Iraq. God told him to leave Ur and go to a place that God would show him. That place was Canaan, now called Israel. God told Abraham that he would give the land to him and to his children. He told Abraham that he would bless him and make his

descendants as numerous as the stars. To us that may not seem a great blessing, but to people in those days it was seen as just about the greatest blessing of all. After all they were still under the instruction God gave to Adam, to multiply and fill the whole earth. God was telling Abraham that he would enable him to do just that. Abraham believed God even though he was childless.

Lot had decided to go with Abraham. But after a while there was not enough room for both of them in the land to feed their flocks and herds. The herdsmen began to quarrel over where to feed the animals. Clearly it was a situation that could get out of hand, and so Abraham, as the senior man, decided to step in and sort out the quarrel.

Now as the senior man the custom of the day was that he had the authority to decide what they should do. Abraham had the right to say to Lot – "Go back to Ur or go somewhere else, for I didn't invite you. This land is not your inheritance; it is mine". Instead he gave some of his inheritance to Lot; he also gave first choice to his nephew. Whatever you choose is yours.

Abraham's choice is an unselfish choice. Abraham chose to put Lot first.

Lot's choice

Lot was, according to Peter, a godly man. But here he did not use godly reasoning to make his choice. We do not read that he tried to refuse Abraham's offer: he could have said: "No, it's your land, you choose; I'll have what's left over.

Lot's choice was based on getting the best for himself. He lifted up his eyes and saw that the plains were lush. There would be plenty of food for his livestock, and thus plenty of food for himself. But it wasn't as if Lot was ever likely to run out of food. He just wanted more. It is quite likely that his wealth in part came from Abraham in the first place. But he pays him scant respect and even less regard and does him a great disservice. He chose the best for himself. This is the choice of a man of God. But his choice turned out to be disastrous, for in the end he was to lose everything he had.

Lot's choice is a selfish choice. Lot chose to put himself first.

You have a choice

You and I have a choice of how we live our life. I am hoping that you have made the first great choice to follow the Lord. Are you a Christian? Holding this book in your hand I hope you are. I trust you have repented of your sin and asked Jesus to forgive you and be your Lord and Saviour. If not, you must do that first.

But assuming you are a Christian, how are you choosing to live your Christian life? You might be surprised at the question. But what I mean is that you can, like Lot, choose to live it selfishly, or like Abraham, you can choose to live it generously. Ask yourself honestly: how selfless are you? Or, how generous are you? Are you prepared to go against the norms of this world and give to others who do not have what you have? Would you ever sit down beside a homeless or needy person and offer them a coffee, a sandwich, and a chat? Do you spend serious time in prayer for the vulnerable in society, the persecuted and the unsaved? What do you do to follow up on those prayers? Do you "give until it hurts". What a difference we could make as Christians in society if we all were as generous as Abraham, not once but continually. Abraham was later to risk his life and all he had to rescue Lot from raiding armies. He remained a generous man.

Wealth and all it brings is not what we live for; but rather if we are not careful, it can be an obstacle to a loving and close relationship with God, and to his people. How do you value and think of what you have today?

Prayer: Lord, help me to consider carefully how I use what I have, and help me to be humbly generous, not seeking to be praised by anyone except you. May what I do be a secret between you and me. Amen.

A mystery unwrapped

The mystery which has been hidden from ages and from generations, but now has been revealed to His saints... the glory of this mystery among the Gentiles, which is Christ in you, the hope of glory.

Colossians 1:26-27

In Colossae, Paul was writing against those who claimed to have a higher knowledge of God, the world, and the meaning of life. After dismantling their theories and showing them to be man-made folly, Paul talks about a real mystery. That mystery has been hidden from the time of Adam; it's been pointed to in the sacrificial system of the Law. It's been glimpsed in the psalms and the prophets, but now the secret is out.

What is the mystery? It is rather like a present that is unwrapped. When I am opening a present, I say "At this moment I don't know what it is". But then the moment of unwrapping arrives, and the secret is out. Paul says that secret is, "*Christ is in you, the hope of glory*".

Christ in you...

Christ is in you. Christ lives in you. Paul has Jesus Christ in him; in his heart, soul, mind, and body. That's the real mystery, not the pretended stuff that was out there in Colossae. Jesus says something of this mystery in John 14:23 when he says: *If anyone loves Me, then he will keep my word; and My Father will love him, and We will come to him and make our home with him.* A Christian is a person in whom God the Father and the Son dwells. How big a mystery is that? If you want a real, amazing mystery, says Paul, look at this. Christ lives in you. God himself lives in the body of every believer. Our castle is the keep of God. Our temple contains the holy of holies where the presence of God is as real as the throne of Heaven itself. Are you aware that God lives in you? What could be greater than that?

78

...the hope...

Why does God live in us? To begin the relationship which will last eternally. It is a deposit guaranteeing the inheritance all Christians have. It therefore is the fuel which drives the engine. Not only do I have a hope, says Paul, I live a hope. I live by hope. *I am crucified with Christ, nevertheless I live, yet not I but Christ lives in me, and the life I live in the flesh I live by faith in the Son of God who loved me and gave himself for me.* This must be our life-driving verse! Paul says in effect: this hope drives me. This hope is my eagerly anticipated expectation; it is my motivation. All I do is done in the context of serving Jesus and looking forward to being with him forever. It is that one day I will see Jesus, be welcomed by Jesus into Heaven and forever, and enter fully into all that he has promised and prepared for me. **_I will_** hear those long-awaited words: *well done, good and faithful servant, enter thou into the joy of thy Lord*. That's the mystery which is revealed in the heart and life of every Christian, for it is true of every Christian. Why does Paul live like he does, makes the choices he does, endures the hardships he does, have the friends he does, travels the miles he does, works as painstakingly as he does? It is all because he is driven on by the certain hope that he pleases Christ now and he will see Christ by and by. His fear of death is gone; the void he has and that we all have as human beings as we long to understand eternal things is filled; the answers to all the big questions are sorted. Paul has a real and living hope in Christ and in Christ alone.

...of Glory.

What will this hope turn into? Glory. Perfection. A new and wonderful life in Heaven. What will Heaven be like? Paradise! No sin, no sorrow; nothing to spoil or mar a perfect relationship with Jesus and his people. How will we get to Heaven? Who will take us there? Where is it? What is Heaven like in environment, in daily life, in relationship to God and to the angels and to other people? What will we see; what will we know? That is the final secret to be revealed, but we know enough to know that what awaits us is worth living and dying for. Jesus calls it Paradise. John says the dwelling of God is now finally, ultimately, and eternally with his people.

But we are given *snapshots of Heaven*[2]. There will be a Resurrection. There will be a new and perfect body and mind. There will be perfect love, peace, and joy. There will be a Marriage. There will be gorgeous clothes. There will be a holy city. Perfect relationships, perfect provision, and a perfect home. That is what awaits the Christian, No wonder Paul calls it the hope of Glory.

Prayer: Lord, help me to realise that you dwell in me, and that my body is your temple. Help me to keep it holy. Help me to live by this hope that you live in me now, and I will live with you in eternity. Amen.

---

[2] Alec Motyer: *After Death*, p.117

81

A new song

And they sang a new song...

Revelation 5:9

Have you ever noticed in the Bible how important songs are? Six times the psalmist says: "sing unto the Lord a new song". Why? A new song was sung when something new and unique had happened. Today, we'll look at four times when a new song was sung.

The song of creation
We are not told this in Genesis, where we're told the creation story, but God tells the greatly suffering Job that when he laid the foundations of the earth, stretched out his measuring line over it, fastened the foundations and laid the cornerstone, the *morning stars sang together, and all the sons of God shouted for joy*.

The Lord is using poetic language, but it is very clear that at creation there was a new song. What was the song about? It was singing the praise of him who made everything from nothing. The angels sang for joy as they beheld the beauty of all that God had made: the cosmos; the earth, with its forests and seas, animals and birds, its fish, and its flowers. What a wonderful time that was. The angels sang for joy then, and sometimes when we see something new in creation, or take a moment to look at the beauty of God's world, it is a joyous moment isn't it?

The song of redemption
The people of Israel left Egypt in a mighty hurry as they had been told to by the Lord. But Pharaoh pursued them with his army with its horses and 600 chariots. After all the disciplining plagues and terrors the Lord had brought upon him and his people, they still wanted their slaves. But the Red Sea parted for Israel and closed over the Egyptians; not one of them was left. As they looked at the bodies on the seashore, Israel went from panic to praise. They sang a new song. God had done something new. Never before and never again do we read of such a deliverance. The song

literally tells the story of what he had done. It was a song of great joy, praise, and hope: *The Lord will reign forever and ever.*

The song of the Saviour

The Christmas story is full of amazing events, but the angels appearing to the shepherds is amongst the greatest. It seems to be like a night like any other. They're settled for the night; the sheep are secure, and they are guarding them as they always did. What they didn't know is that a baby has been born nearby in Bethlehem. That's a place they have no desire to go to. Its chock-full of people obeying Caesar, who has ordered a census of all the empire. There's no place to stay, barely a place to move or breathe. But all is calm on the hillsides until suddenly in front of them an angel, telling them of Jesus' birth. Before they have time to catch their breath, a host of angels are singing a new song: *"Glory to God in the highest, and on earth peace, goodwill toward men!"*

We cannot imagine their fear, their amazement, and their wonder. But to their credit these shepherds go and worship the one who is the Shepherd-King: to them belongs the honour of becoming the first human worshippers of the new-born King. The kingdom is heralded in.

The song of eternity

In Revelation chapter 5 we have a final, new song: *"You are worthy to take the scroll, and to open its seals; for You were slain and have redeemed us to God by Your blood. Out of every tribe and tongue and people and nation and have made us kings and priests to our God; and we shall reign on the earth."*

The final new song is singing of the end of all things. All the previous new songs are bound up in the last new song of Jesus the Lamb of God who alone is worthy of all worship. He is the one who spoke creation into being, who brought redemption for Israel, salvation for his people and is

83

coming again to take his people home. When you sing to God, have in mind these four songs that mark the four epochs of Bible history, a history you are part of if you are one of His.

Prayer: Lord, help me to always enjoy singing to you. Help me to sing of your creation, redemption, salvation, and final glory Amen.

What does blessed mean?
Blessed are…

Matthew 5:3

In Matthew 5 we have what are called The Beatitudes; so-called after the Latin translation *"beati sunt"*, which literally translates as "Blessed are". Jesus begins his teaching about what the kingdom of Heaven is, who is part of it, and what it is like to live in the kingdom.

The first word Jesus uses is "Blessed". *"Jesus came into the world to bless us"* (Acts 3: 26), says Matthew Henry. To be blessed is, simply put, to be happy. But what sort of happiness are we talking about?

What does "Blessed" mean?
Seven Psalms start with "Blessed", and it always denotes that certain people are blessed by God for what they are in character, or what having that character leads to.

Psalm 1: who walks not this way, but that way.

Psalm 34: whose transgression is covered.

Psalm 41: who considers the poor (cf James)

Psalm 112: who fears the Lord.

Psalm 119: undefiled in the way.

Psalm 128: who fears the Lord.

Psalm 144: be the Lord my strength.

Psalm 1 gives us the key: blessed is the man who walks… It has a double emphasis. Blessed comes from a root word which means to go long, to make large. In other words, to go straight. This blessing is a long, large, continuous thing. The word-picture is that of walking out into a large space. If you exit a dark cave or tunnel into the light, with all the warmth of the sun beaming down on you, that is the kind of happiness the psalmist speaks of.

The pilgrim in Psalm 1 is walking on in the ways of God. He is happily walking in God's sunshine. The righteous walk is his blessing and God pronounces the blessing on him. Blessing, and blessedness are rife through-out the Bible. Without wanting to turn this into an English language lesson, *"blessed,"* can be a verb, a noun, and an adjective. As a verb, it means **to bless**; Mary was blessed by the angel when he brought the astounding news that she was to be the mother of the Messiah, and it was echoed by Elizabeth. Jesus blessed the loaves and fish before the miraculous feeding of the 5,000 and 4,000 respectively.

As a noun it means **to praise**, to thank. The psalmist blesses God, as do Paul and many other writers. Psalm 103:1: *Bless the Lord, O my soul, and all that is within me bless his holy name*. Psalm 104:1; *Bless the Lord, O my soul. O Lord my God you are very great.* The Psalmist here, as he does many times elsewhere, blesses the Lord for his goodness, greatness, and kindness, something we should do every day. We should not forget his benefits..

But in Matthew 5, we are seeing this word as an adjective. As well as the Beatitudes, we read this in the Psalms, and seven times in Revelation, where the word is used to describe the character of the person who is trusting, reading, meditating on God's word, or who is watching for him to come, or who is dying as a Christian and taking part in the resurrection. The person who is blessed is being blessed by the Lord for doing something, for being something, and it is a blessing that is **given**: it is bestowed by God. Jesus is saying God is blessing you, God is making your way straight, he is in the act of walking you out into the sunshine, into a large and beautiful place. Ultimately it is a picture of salvation.

Who is blessed?
At first sight these so-called Beatitudes seem anything but a blessing. To be blessed in this large, and amazing way we need to be poor in spirit, to mourn, to be meek and so on. It doesn't sound that positive, does it? Yet Psalm 72:12-14. Isaiah 11:4-5 and 61: 1-4 all prefigure this teaching and are really a prophecy of Jesus who bestows these blessings.

Who is blessed? Those in whose life all these characteristics exist. They are the true citizens of the kingdom. *All* Christians are <u>all</u> of these things. Thomas Watson writes that this blessing: *brings supreme good... is of supreme quality... is delicious... plentiful... all fulness... perfect...and eternal.*[3]

Christian, the Beatitudes are not a new set of commandments, but a statement of what God has saved and called you to be.

Prayer: Lord, help me to thank you always for your blessings. Help me to grow in grace and display these graces in my life today. Amen.

---

[3] The Beatitudes, p.29

Spiritual poverty

Blessed are the poor in spirit.

Matthew 5:3

As said yesterday, the Beatitudes seem absurd contradictions don't they? How can a happy man be poor, mourning, or meek? Yet, once we understand what blessedness is, we can see what Jesus is saying. In fact, the words he uses in this beatitude are very strong words. Blessed are the poor in spirit. The word poor means a cringing beggar, a pauper. The world, and the prosperity gospel movement, say "blessed are the rich". But it is not so.

At Flatford Mill there is a 17th century house called Bridge Cottage. Inside there is a depiction of one of the last families to live and work the area.

 This family were nine people in a very small space. People had lived there for 200 years, farming the land, and using the river. Even now, the Mill and the River Stour seem timeless. But in the 1890s, the railways were taking away the trade of the barges, which took goods to and from the ports along the River Stour. Income was dropping. The farmer, who owned the land, and their home, was running out of money. He had re-mortgaged his house, but the tenant's home was part of the collateral. If he sold their house, they'd be homeless. They would have nowhere to go, no-one to house them. The pressure was great. Where would they live? How would they eat? Begging might be the only option. A terrible poverty.

And when Jesus is talking about a poverty of spirit, he means a real poverty. Our spirit is the vital us, the soul, the inner being, that which God breathed into Adam in the Garden, it. To be poor in spirit means that we recognise that, as far as our relationship with God is concerned, we are bankrupt.

Bankrupt before God

In Luke 18, Jesus spoke a parable because there were those who trusted in themselves that they were righteous. They were convinced that God would accept them. One like them, stood up and told God all he had done. He had tithed his money, fasted, kept the Law. What a great guy I must be in your sight. We can almost imagine him giving God a book which listed all his good deeds. There were good deeds, no doubt about it. But God takes that book, reads each entry, and tears out, page by page all the good deeds, saying this won't count, nor this, nor this. And as he does so, picture this man, confident of Heaven. See his confidence begins to wane; he then gets angry, then frightened, then, in despair, he falls to his knees. Nothing counts. The book is empty. He is bankrupt. His hopes of Heaven are crushed. Why? He did not do his acts of righteousness for God; he did them for himself. He did them to boast. He did them to show God how easy his standards were, and how he had conquered the mountain, so to speak.

The other man in the parable is bankrupt. He is poor, bereft, and hopeless. What does he do? His head is bowed to the king. His eyes are on the floor. He beats his chest, as if to save the king from doing it. This man is a sinner. He does the only thing he can: he begs for mercy.

And that is what it is to be poor in spirit. Such a person is blessed. Do you see yourself not as a good person who's done a few bad things, but as a person who has no hope of earning any favour with God by your life, and, like a beggar, you have fallen to your knees and begged for mercy? That is why it is impossible for a person to become a Christian by themselves. It is more possible to thread a camel though the eye of a needle. You and I have nothing to pay the king of Heaven for entry into his kingdom. We have no passport. If you know that, believe that, and are ready to humble yourself before God, then you are poor in spirit. Jesus says to the poor in spirit, and to them only, theirs is the kingdom of Heaven. We cannot storm the doors of Heaven by our arrogant self-righteousness. Jesus said to the Laodicean church, you think you are so rich, so good. You think I am pleased with your acts of goodness. But I hate them. Like lukewarm food I will spit you out of my mouth. You are miserable, wretched, poor, blind, and naked.

And the point is that Jesus is talking to Christians. He is teaching us who have come for mercy. We must stay poor in spirit. The Laodiceans forgot where they came from and so, very easily, can we. Blessed <u>are</u>. Today and every day let us walk before God in poverty of spirit, recognising where we came from, and having no desire to be what we once were.

Prayer: Lord, help me to never rely on my good deeds to get to Heaven, nor boast of them to you or others. Help me to remain every day, poor in spirit. Then I will know your blessing. Amen.

How great is our God?

Bless the Lord o my soul! O Lord my God, you are very great.

Psalm 104:1

The psalmist bows before God in an attitude of awe and wonder. This psalm is all about God's greatness. But what exactly is greatness?

Greatness is usually a comparative: we talk about great men and great women; we usually mean that they are great in comparison to us. They stand out from us. They stand above us. But God's greatness is above comparison. His greatness is absolute. No-one can be compared to him (Isaiah 40:18). He is unique. What he has done, continues to do and will do cannot be spoken about in the same breath as another, for no-one is in his league. How great is our God?

God is eternal: He has always been here

I have written before that the Bible never seeks to prove the existence of God. It simply states that He does. Genesis 1:1 *In the beginning God created the Heavens and the earth.* We are considering someone who has always existed. In Hebrews 13:8 we read: *Jesus Christ, the same yesterday and today and forever.* Think about that. The greatest of friends and family members leave us. But God is always here. He will always be.

God is the Creator: He made everything

This theme occupies much of Psalm 104. But look at the opening verses of Psalm 19, as well. Evolution and theistic evolution are Satan's master-lies (see Exodus 20:11, 31:17). In six days, from nothing, God created everything.. And as you come to God in prayer, set your heart and mind to deliberately speak to God; think about him creating the world. Think about the hands that, *"flung stars into space."*[4] Think about the sun going round the circuit of the earth, at exactly where it must be or else we would either freeze or burn. It is too much to fully understand, but here is God, waiting to talk with us, the one whose word created all we know.

---

[4] Line from the hymn *"From Heaven you came"* by Graham Kendrick

God is a person we know

Luther called God *"Deus absconditus"*, the Hidden one, because the greatness of God is so unfathomable, we cannot hope to know, understand, or "pigeon-hole" him as we want to. He is just too vast. The Heavens cannot contain him, so how can we "take him in"? But, at the same time, he is no stranger. That is because he has taken the trouble to make himself known. This is why reading the Bible is so important. We pray, we sing, we worship, and we listen to the God who speaks to us. He reveals himself to us in his word. He tells us about himself. He, the one who inhabits eternity, comes down to our level. Isn't it true that we come to know someone as they reveal what they are like? So, it is with God. But how does God speak and what does he say, and how does that help me get to know him better? In short, the whole Bible tells us of God, but let us look at some extracts.

We've already cited Psalm 19 which tells us that the *Heavens declare the glory of God*. This psalm gives us a glimpse of His power, splendour, and vastness. Go to Psalm 93 which gives us another look at his power. *The Lord reigns… The Lord is clothed with majesty… he is girded* (belted) *with strength…The Lord on high is mightier than many waters.*

Even a look at the names God uses for himself tell us so much about him. El means being first; Elohim means a power that strikes fear; Elyon, God is most high. Adonai is the master or the judge, Shaddai, denotes a mother's protective love (Psalm 91:1). The most used, Yahweh (over 5000 times), means "to be".

We know that God knows all things, is all-wise and fills all of his creation. When you approach God, spend some time thinking on his greatness. God is able to do anything he chooses to do. He is able to hear and save to the uttermost any human being. He is able to do abundantly above all we could ever ask or imagine. This is the limitless power, capability, and majesty of God. And you and I are invited to come to him, day or night through the living way that Jesus has made through his death on the Cross.

Prayer: Lord, help me to reflect on your greatness, and what that means when I see the world, and my world sometimes, in chaos. Help me today to put my trust in your greatness. Amen.

Hanging on in the dark

But David strengthened himself in the Lord his God.

I Samuel 30:6

David was in a difficult phase of his life. Sometimes life seems to throw us a continual "bad hand". In those times when wave after wave of attacks from the enemy seem to drown us in sorrow, confusion and doubt, it is harder to remember, calmly, that God is leading us even in those times. David wrote in Psalm 23 about the Lord who led him into the valley of the shadow of death and out of it again into the place of delight.

But David at this point was neither shepherd nor king. He was being pursued by Saul the king of Israel, who hated him and was jealous of him, even though David had only done both him and the kingdom great good by defeating Goliath and the Philistine army. He went from place to place seeking refuge but found none. With his band of discontents now swelled to a lean, mean fighting force of 600 men, David bargained with Achish, king of Gath who had driven him away earlier (Psalm 34) for a city to rule under his kingship. Achish gave him Ziklag, a little city southwest of Israel, and it was out of sight and reach of Saul and far enough away from the Philistines to not worry about them either.

But David plays a dangerous game, for he goes quietly about the area to the south of Ziklag towards Egypt, annihilating small cities of the ancient peoples who lived there, leaving no survivors. Whilst Achish believed David was fighting Israelite cities in the north, making himself abhorrent to the Israelites, David was removing future opposition. David even went as far as to line up with Philistines against Saul at Aphek but was sent away by concerned Philistine chiefs who thought he could turn against them.

When he arrived home from Aphek, David discovered that the Amalekites, whom he had been raiding had in turn raided him. Everything was gone that could be taken; everything was burned that couldn't. His warriors were so furious with him that they planned to stone him. We're not told why they blamed David as such, but clearly David's unwise policy now came back to bite him, hard. We read: *Then David and the people who were with him lifted up their voices and wept, until they had no more power to weep*. They literally cry themselves to a standstill. So, put yourself if you can, in David's place. He has no home, no family, (his parents he had sent to Moab), no possessions, no future (it seems), and now his life is in danger:

David was greatly distressed, for the people spoke of stoning him, because the soul of all the people was grieved... But David strengthened himself in the LORD his God. As Amos says (5:19), it's a bit like the man

who escaped from the lion, met a bear, ran from the bear to home, to be bitten by a snake!

I wonder how well you do when the world falls in. Satan desperately tries to get us to blame God as he did with Job. Our own self-centred hearts get angry with God, and the world tut-tuts and says, "this is proof there is no God", for how could [a] God [of love] allow this?

David strengthened himself in the Lord his God. That word strengthened means to fasten upon, or to seize. David turned to God in his trouble and held on tightly! He reminded himself that the Lord was *his* God. The Lord had chosen him to be his own. He had chosen him to be king. God had made him promises. David reminded himself that the reality that he could not see was greater than the reality he could. He turns to God and seeks his will. He calls for the priest to bring the ephod and he prays to God for an answer to the situation. God tells him what to do, but it required great courage to do it. David proves God's faithfulness and love for him, and he rescues the entire collection of captives alive and unharmed.

We have a greater priest than David had; the Lord Jesus Christ, and we have his word. But He is not to be treated as a *"magical Genie who we rub up to when the going gets tough"*[5]. Rather, he is the awesome, unchanging, ever-loving God who loved me and gave himself for me. He is my God. And my God shall supply all your needs through Christ Jesus. God never changes. He is to be trusted; His word is to be trusted. His love is to be trusted. Trust in Him in the dark and hold on tight.

Prayer: Lord, thank you that you never change. Help me to seize hold of you in prayer and in faith when I am hanging on in the dark. Amen.

---

[5] Dale Ralph Davis: *I Samuel*, p.312

Be merciful

Blessed are the merciful, for they shall obtain mercy.

The word "mercy" translates as "active compassion", or "a heart touched at the pain of another". The merciful enter into the miseries of another[6]. The basis of your relationship with God is mercy. God has had mercy on you. Jesus alludes to Psalm 18:25, *With the merciful you will show yourself merciful.* And the word *"merciful"* here is only used on one other occasion in the New Testament; in Hebrews 2:17, where Jesus is described as being a *"merciful High Priest"*: as Jesus knows the misery of being tempted, as we are tempted; his merciful (ness) is born out of experience, and that lends to the compassion he shows us, for he knows what we go through.

The parable of the two servants in Matthew 18:23-35 illustrates the mercy Jesus speaks of very clearly. Peter asks: *how often shall I forgive my brother?* Is he referring to his brother? Was Andrew an annoying little brother? Or was Peter talking about people in general. But here is the rub: people are annoying aren't they? People get on your nerves don't they? People hurt you, don't they? You can think of one or more people who have hurt you, or who are hurting your right now. And what do you naturally do? You think about what you would like to do to pay them back; to get justice, to get revenge. And Jesus knows what that feeling is like. He was tempted to think those thoughts (Hebrews 2:17 tells us). So, what does he tell us to do?

Imagine, he says, that you are this servant that owed the master 10,000 talents. Let us set that in context: one talent = 6000 denarii; one denarius = one day's wage (Matthew 20:2), so: 10,000 talents = **60 million days labour.**

So, in other words, a debt he could never repay. All the master could do was to sell him, and his family, into slavery and get something back. But

---

[6] Preachers Homiletic Commentary, Matthew, p.86

the servant begs for mercy. The master has mercy, and he freely forgives him.

How do you think that servant felt? How should he have felt? Relieved yes, and much more. He should have been crying for joy, being so thankful, a bit like Dickens' Scrooge when he wakes up after his nightmares to find he is alive and he straightaway in joy goes and gives to the poor. An amazed, grateful, thankful heart. God's mercy inspires mercy in you.

If that servant had had those feelings we would not read what happens next: instead of gratitude he goes and hunts down a fellow servant who owes him 100 denarii. Now, it is a sizeable debt. A 100 days' wages. Let's not overlook that it was a real, large debt that was owed. This servant was guilty. This servant must pay. But what is the point here? Context. Instead of being grateful for being freed from his unpayable debt, the first servant blamed the other for his problem. Instead of owning up to his own folly and sin, the servant looked at the other and despised him. Mercy demanded that the first servant should, out of his own abundant store  of joy and gratitude, forgive the second. But, he had no mercy. And those who show no mercy, receive no mercy. Jesus answers Peter with these solemn words: *"So My Heavenly Father also will do to you if each of you, from his heart, does not forgive his brother his trespasses."* Be merciful out of your store of amazement and gratitude, that Jesus forgave you. Paul writes *be kind to one another, tender-hearted, forgiving one another, even as God in Christ forgave you*. I Corinthians 13 states, love keeps no record of wrong.

So, how do you cope with hurt, injustice, pain that someone inflicted whether it be deliberate or not? The old you, the natural you wants justice.

But you owed God a debt you couldn't pay: the debt of your sin, breaking God's Law an untold number of times. But Jesus paid the debt; he paid it all. Now, someone owes you a debt they may not be able to pay: perhaps money, perhaps forgiveness. But since Jesus has paid your debt, you must pay his by cancelling it, by reckoning that debt gone, by forgiving him from your heart, by forgetting that debt ever existed. So, being merciful is an active thing, something we learn to do, something we practise. It is not natural, but it is essential. Without forgiveness the kingdom of God cannot function. Forgive whole-heartedly. Forgive often. Forgive quickly. Forgive with joy. Blessed (by God) are the merciful, for they shall obtain mercy.

Prayer: Lord, thank you for your unbelievable mercy. Help me to see that the debts I'm owed are so small. Help me to show mercy. Amen.

104

How to see God clearly

Blessed are the pure in heart, for they shall see God.

Matthew 5: 8

Purity of heart is an essential part of being a disciple of Jesus Christ. Why is it so hard to be pure? Because we are naturally selfish. This blessing is the core of our Christian life. Psalm 18: 25, *with the pure you will show yourself pure*. God expects purity. His holiness demands it. We cannot be pure naturally. We must learn, study, strive after, work at it, being pure in heart. Literally, pure means clean and clear, like sparkling water from a Scottish babbling brook coming down from the mountains. I went for a paddle once in it - ouch! It was ice cold, yet it was so clear and beautifully clean, I was drawn to it.

But purity is not naivety, nor is it the same as innocence. This purity is that of being washed clean after being dirty, like the Psalmist being taken up out of the horrible pit, out of the miry clay. To put it as a scientific equation: purity is clean + power: it cleans what it touches. That is Bible purity.

But what do we mean by purity of heart? It means the mind, the thoughts, the deep recesses of us. It is the bit we see and know, and hope no-one else does. So, Jesus is talking about purity in the *Eros* sense, but he is also talking about purity in the sense of honesty, integrity, and motive. We must have pure motives, pure looks, pure thoughts: we must have integrity.

Job said: "*I have made a covenant with my eyes, not to look* [lustfully] *on a girl*". We do well to emulate him. The "blessed" disciple is to guard his eyes, mind, motives, and speech. How do we do that? Many Christians decide to give themselves rules. "I will do this, but not that. I will go here, but not there." That usually leads to two problems: legalism and self-righteousness; the former to not purity but fossilisation, and the latter to judging and looking down upon others. My Nanna was strictly forbidden to go to the pictures by her parents. Those who did were deemed to be a "lesser sort"!

How do we live a pure life? How are we to bask in the sunshine of God's pleasure and approval? Not by legalism but by love. I need to be satisfied with God, with what he has given me, and what he has made me. That is so much better than rule-keeping. It is far nobler, positive, and helpful. It will make 1000 decisions without feeding your pride. James 4:1-7:

Where do wars and fights come from among you? Do they not come from your desires for pleasure that war in your members? You lust and do not have. You murder and covet and cannot obtain. You fight and war. Yet you do not have... do you think that the Scripture says in vain, "The Spirit who dwells in us yearns jealously"?

What is the fighting and warring all about? It is that we want what is not ours; we want what we should not and cannot have. See the passion in the verbs here. Fight, war, desire, covet. These things take us away from God. These things if we walk after, cuddle up to, and sit down and enjoy, will kill our friendship with God (Psalm 1). God is still the same jealous God that he was over Israel. He will not share his beloved with another, to use the imagery of the Song of Songs. Stop looking at what others have, whether it be their possessions, family, looks, power, money, and so on. All these can be taken away at a stroke. Yes, in this life, some will have more than others. Jesus himself speaks of the master giving ten talents to one, five to another, and so on. But who had to account for the most? Who had to work the hardest? The one who had the most. To those to whom much is given, much will be required. It is not the soft or easy option to have much of this world's goods. This is why the richest, wisest man on earth cried out saying: *Give me neither poverty nor riches, but food enough for me* (Proverbs 30:8). For where your treasure is there your heart will be also.

"*When I awake*", says the psalmist, "*I will be satisfied with your likeness*". That should be true every morning. I am satisfied with what God has made me, has given me, where he has taken me. I am satisfied with where I am going, with what is in store for me. And purity of heart implies a single-mindedness which is all about pleasing God in what I do, and the way I do it, not to be seen by others.

And the reward? It is to see God; Job knew he would (19:26-27). If we long for God now, how wonderful it will be when we see him. That is the *perfect love which casts out fear* [of death].

Prayer: Lord, help me to be satisfied with you and all you have given me. Help my purity to powerful and cleansing Amen.

One thing

One thing I have desired of the Lord, that will I seek:
That I may dwell in the house of the Lord all the days of my life,
to behold the beauty of the Lord, and to inquire in His temple.

Psalm 27:4

Have you ever had anyone say to you *"you only had one job"*, *"you only had to do one thing*!" It's normally in the context of either scolding or mocking that you hear it. A football defender just has to clear the ball, but he miskicks it, or a husband (me!) has to remember one thing to get at the shop and he comes back with something entirely different. One thing... At school, one thing you have to do is your homework. Later on, one thing you have to do is pass your exams. Later on, the "one thing" you want is a husband or a wife, a career, a house, and so on. And there is nothing wrong in human beings having a focus on getting that "one thing" in and of itself.

But, if you were to ask David what his one thing was, and we are not sure when he wrote this psalm, items on his agenda reasonably might be: to not be a shepherd, to escape Saul, to be king, or to have a bigger kingdom. And, in fact, he received those things. And it is a sure thing that when you have these things, you do not wish to give them up. But it is clear that David was content to wait for God to sort those things out in his good time. But whatever and wherever he was when he wrote this psalm, we are not left wondering what it is that David would ask for.

David wanted one thing: to know the Lord. This is what he writes of in this psalm. But although it is one thing it has several parts:
Firstly, David wants to *dwell in the house of the Lord all the days of my life*. Literally David is earnestly asking to sit down with the Lord. It could also translate as to move in with Him. David wants the closest possible intimacy with God. Physically to dwell in the temple

was impossible, for only the High Priest could go into the presence of the Lord and that once a year and that with blood. But David shows his heart and it's not the first time. In Psalm 23:6 he says: *I will dwell in the house of the LORD. Forever.* There he is much more definite, and of course that is where is right now.

To behold the beauty of the Lord. In the house of the Lord stood the amazing ark of the covenant where the Lord dwelt symbolically; it was the token of his presence with Israel. David wanted to stay there to reflect on God's character, his love, holiness, and person. He wanted to take in all that God was, and all that God had done for him.

To inquire in his Temple. David wanted to spend time praying with God. This word inquire literally means to plough, and figuratively to inspect and admire God. But the praying here is less about asking for things, and more about worshipping God. And in using the word Temple, David is being prophetic, for the temple wasn't yet built. There was still the temporary tabernacle. But David had laid plans for the Temple to be built and he longed for the day it would be finished. It would be where God was honoured, worshipped, and acknowledged as the true God of his people.

David's longing is both moving and prophetic. The Temple was built, rebuilt, but finally destroyed. The ultimate Temple is Jesus Christ, through whom the Temple curtain was torn in two and access for sinners was purchased by his blood. David's longing came true perfectly when he was called home. But God's house is where God dwells. And whilst it's true that the Heaven of Heavens cannot contain him, God condescends to dwell with his people. Not merely in their midst, as he did in the wilderness Tabernacle, where he was in the centre of where the tribes camped, nor in the magnificent Temple of Solomon where he symbolically lived amongst his people, but now he spiritually dwells in the heart, soul, and life of each one of his people, who are born again by the Holy Spirit and lived in by the Father and the Son. The whole Trinity resides in the lives of each one of us if we are His. Do we long for the felt presence of God as David did? Do we want to "move in" with God, to be so close to him, that nothing gets in between? David was called a man after God's own heart. Are we?

Prayer: Lord, help me to have David's longing to dwell with, gaze upon and inquire for you. Help me to not rest until I have your felt presence with me. Amen.

God's love story

Take your servant under your wing.

Ruth 3:9

Most of us like a love story with a happy ending. It gives that feeling of this is how it ought to be. If Ruth's book were merely a love story, it would be a good read. Here are the five parts to a great story: the characters, the setting, the plot, the twist, and the reconciliation (happy ending). My young schoolchildren and I loved to make up and write a chapter a day of our new stories. But Ruth's story is true, and it pictures God's love for his people as well as gives a glimpse into his eternal plan of redemption. It is a great story. In tribute to its significance, Ruth was read at the Feast of Weeks i.e. Pentecost. It is set in the time of the Judges; and since Boaz was King David's great grandfather, and David was born around 1040BC, a guessed time of around 1150BC seems plausible.

Ruth's story

A man called Elimelech decides to leave Bethlehem for Moab to escape the famine in Israel. Tragically, Elimelech dies, but the family stay in Moab, for his sons meet and marry Moabite women. Mahlon marries Orpah and Chilion marries Ruth. Both sons die, and Naomi (meaning pleasant) has the bitter (Mara) job of burying her two sons. She returns to Bethlehem, she says, empty. But, in fact, she has Ruth.

The opening chapter is all about the choices that the protagonists in the story make. So far, none of the choices have been wise or profitable, except the last one. Ruth chooses Naomi, her people, and her God. She gives up all to go to where God's people and God's promised presence will be.

Ruth meets Boaz. He is impressed with her modesty and integrity. She goes to glean in the fields for Naomi. Boaz decides to protect her. He is a relative of the family, a kinsman. It's an

114

interesting word because it sets the scene for what follows.

Then we have the plot twisting and turning. There is an etiquette to get round: Naomi sets the plan up, almost Shakespeare-like. It is a surprising and dangerous plan, but Ruth obeys Naomi, although Naomi is risking Ruth's reputation.

But the happy ending comes. Boaz and Ruth marry. We then are told implicitly why this book is in God's canon: not just the story of love and type, but that Ruth plays a part in God's eternal plan, to send his Son to be the redeemer of Israel, and the world. Boaz is shown to be a type of Christ, for the Kingsman-redeemer must be a blood relative, be able to pay the price, look with kindness upon the poor and needy (2:5), redeem people and property 4:5, and be willing to redeem. Jesus is all that for us.

What does this story teach us?
The scriptures do not criticize the decision of Elimelech and Naomi, but the stark fact is that they made a pragmatic choice, rather than believe the promises of God. The rest of Bethlehem's residents survived, so surely, they would have done. Perhaps they concluded that since all Israel was sinning and forsaking God, they could not be sure that the famine would end. Nevertheless, the decision cost them dearly. Naomi's spiritual state is indicated in her lament, in her advice she gives to Ruth and Orpah, and even in the ruse she concocts to get Ruth and Boaz together. She is a pragmatist: she knows the scriptures but decides that God needs a hand. She could have ruined Ruth's reputation. The end never justifies the means: we work from scriptural principles, not ever from pragmatism.

Ruth's pledge is so spiritual we could almost use it as a gospel prayer. When we come to faith in Christ, we know that the Lord will never leave us nor forsake us. He will never ask us to leave either. Wherever we go, He goes, and where we live, study, work, move to, and where we retire, He will be there. God's people are our people, their God is our God, and when we die the Lord is there too and will carry us to Heaven.

Ruth is a type of the Gentile Church. As a Moabite, the Law excluded her, but grace saved her. The Law excludes us also, but the grace of the Lord Jesus saves us. Take your servant under your wing is really a proposal of marriage. We are the bride of Christ, loved, chosen, bought, and preserved by him, to be in a mystical union with him for ever.

Prayer: Lord, thank you that I am part of your great love story. Help me to realise that I am greatly loved by you. Help me to love you in return, by my gratitude and my obedience. Amen.

Thoughtful praise of God

Proclaim the praises of him who called you out of darkness into his marvellous light.

I Peter 2:9

We are to be a proclaiming people. What does that mean? Proclaiming the praises (meaning God's virtues, or qualities), is to mark how wonderful God is. Once we have grasped (something of) that, we use what we have learned to praise him. This is thoughtful praise of God.

God's "Godness"

Firstly, think about God always existing. He needs nothing to exist. We need air, water, food, warmth, and shelter. God needs none of those things.

Secondly, everything that exists is totally dependent on God. We pray and ask God for things because we need his help. God needs no help.

Thirdly, God is able to exist without us, but we are not able to exist without him. He is completely independent of us all. Nebuchadnezzar (the world's greatest emperor) was humbled by God: *He does whatever he pleases with the powers of Heaven and the peoples of the earth. No-one can hold back his hand or say to him: "What have you done?"* (Daniel 4:35).

The Trinity

This is a fact that is hard to grasp. God is Father, Son, and Holy Spirit. One God, three persons. They all agree. They are all divine. They are united. But they have different roles. God the Father purposed to have a people who would know him, love him, and spend eternity with him. His Son, the Lord Jesus Christ, died to make that possible, taking away our sins. The Holy Spirit regenerates us (we are born again, or from above, John 3). The Son is given the highest place, by the Father; the Spirit is self-effacing.

Unchanging

God never changes his personality, his character, or his purposes. Malachi 3:6: *I am the Lord; I do not change*. God's promises do not change, nor will they fail. We make promises and change our mind or maybe are unable to carry them out. But God is never like this. When he says he will save to the uttermost all those who come to God through Jesus, he means it and is able to do it. When he says that all who come to him he will never cast out, he means it. When he says he will send the Holy Spirit to dwell in the hearts of all who believe, then that is what happens. When he says he will come again to judge the world, create a new Heaven and earth in which only righteousness will dwell and dwell with his people, that is exactly what he means, and we can entrust our eternal future on those promises.

But there is more

There is even more to praise God for. He is perfect. There is no fault in him. The kindest human being you have known has imperfect motives, abilities, and understanding, but "as for God, his way is perfect". You will never catch God being selfish, or unfaithful. Never is he unkind or rude. The fruits of the Spirit are perfected in him: love, joy, peace, longsuffering, kindness, good-ness, faithfulness, gentleness, and self-control.

Think about, for example, the necessity of the God with unlimited power needing self-control. What would it be like if (I say it reverently) God lost his temper with us? And however we provoke him, He will never do that.
Think of the gentleness of God. This vast, incomparable person, who with a word can, and did, create light out of darkness, is so gentle with us. David wrote, *he knows our frame, he remembers that we are dust* (Psalm 103:14). We are so breakable, so fragile, so easily hurt. He is the gentle, all-powerful God who delights to come to us and commune with us.

Think of his love. Endless acres of print have been occupied by writers on love. But the Bible describes the deepest love of all. *Behold, what manner of love the Father has bestowed upon us that we should be called the children of God* (I John 3:1). *How precious also are your thoughts to me O*

God! How great the sum of them! If I should count them, they should be more in number than the sand. (Psalm 139:17-18). God's love is proven by his action. *God so loved the world that he gave his only begotten Son, that whosoever believes on him shall not perish but have everlasting life.* Think on these things today. Talk to someone else, if you can, about them. You'll often be surprised at where the conversation goes and how the blessing of God comes. We are to be thoughtful proclaimers of him who loves us with an everlasting love.

Prayer: Lord, thank you that you never change. Help me today to think about all that you are. Help me to be a proclaimer. Amen.

The Lord is coming again

For you know perfectly that the day of the Lord so comes as a thief in the night: Therefore, let us not sleep, as others, but let us watch and be sober.

I Thessalonians 5:2-6

It may seem a surprising question, but does the Second Coming of the Lord have any bearing in your daily life? In the first letter to the Thessalonians, it is quite clear that Paul expects them (and us) to live their whole lives with this expectation at the forefront of their minds and actions. Of course, they were first century Christians and everything about the gospel was new. We are 21st century Christians and the doctrine of the Second Coming may seem much less real and less impending. It is easy for

us to let this all-important event slip from our minds. But the fact is that every new day brings that final day closer. We have less time to reach the lost than we did yesterday. We will have even less time tomorrow. What we do in the work of the kingdom is what will count in the end. To that end our lives must reflect this astounding, world-ending event.

What is going to happen?

On a certain day, which God the Father has already put in his diary, the Lord Jesus will, unexpectedly, descend from Heaven with a great shout. Paul likens his coming to be as swift, decisive, and invasive as a thief. For some it be a terrible day, for others a day of unbridled joy. He will come with his angels. The Christians who have died already will come with him, and those who are alive when he returns will be caught up to meet him in the air. The existing Heavens and earth will be rolled up like an old garment, and all mankind will be summoned to appear before the judgement seat of Christ. Those who trusted him as their Saviour will join him in the new creation; those who did not will be sent away to everlasting punishment.

Why is this important?

In the verses above Paul, brings several things to our attention. First, there are those who are living as if this day will never come. They may have various beliefs in Jesus, or none, or they may hold other religious beliefs. To them, that day will bring the biggest shock they could never have imagined. The fear and hopelessness they will feel cannot be written down. Just as they think all is well, Paul says, destruction rains down upon them. We must pray for them.

If we are living in the light of that day, then we will not be surprised, but there is the challenge for us. Are we watching for that day? Are we looking for it? Are we being sober? Sober living reminds us that the things of this world are temporary. We need to constantly evaluate whether what we are doing is in fact profitable. Are we wasting our time, or using it wisely? Are we letting our light so shine before men that they are seeing our good works and glorifying our Father in Heaven? Are we bringing eternity into their minds? Being sons of the light brings with it a great responsibility.

How do I live with the Second Coming in mind?

Paul has said (3:13) that we should live holy lives, waiting for Jesus' coming. Whilst we work, watch, and wait with great hope, we must pray. We must thank God constantly for our hope. We are looking forward to a new life in Christ, which will be perfect, wonderful, glorious, and unending. We must ask earnestly that the Lord's death will save even more people. Let us bring those we know and love who are not saved before the Lord in prayer, with great fervour asking him to save them. Let us ask how we can be a partner in that work. That may seem daunting, but it is important. As we work, we will find the Lord working, for that is what partnership entails.

Let us pray for preachers of God's word, our pastors, and preachers. Let us pray for mission work. Let us get involved in some way, praying with others very specifically for these things, so that they are at the forefront of

123

our minds. As we are able let us support this work with our time, gifts, and finances. Above all let us keep on taking this work seriously in the light of the second coming, for we shall reap in due season if we faint not.

Prayer: Lord, thank you that I have a sure and certain promise from you that you are coming again. Help me to focus on that glorious day, and what the new creation will be like. Help me to revel in the wonderful hope that wonderful day will bring. Help me to pray for the lost to be saved and help me to do so persistently, knowing you will save all who call on you, all you have loved from before the foundation of the world. Amen.

Thank you for Reading

About Gary Stevens

Gary Stevens is also the author of:

- The Pilgrim's Psalmgress
- Daily Progress
- Ordinary Pilgrams Extraordinary Progress

All these are available on Amazon

You can find out more information about Gary and his books on his website: garybstevens.co.uk

126

Printed in Great Britain
by Amazon

37807104R00076